Fashion is not just about clothes,
but also the stories of the designers.

FASHIONARY

ISBN 978-988-77110-2-5
SN 50LV152105PBHL
Designed and published in Hong Kong
by Fashionary International Ltd
Printed in China

If you have any feedback of the book, please don't hesitate to send it to feedback@fashionary.org

🄵 @ fashionary
🄸 @ fashionary
🄟 @ fashionary

Fashionary Team

THE LIVES OF
50 FASHION LEGENDS
Visual biographies of the world's greatest designers

FASHIONARY

CONTENTS

Coco Chanel
14

Cristóbal Balenciaga
16

Christian Dior
18

Pierre Balmain
20

Emilio Pucci
22

Pierre Cardin
24

Hubert de Givenchy
26

Mary Quant
32

Sonia Rykiel
34

Valentino Garavani
36

Oscar de la Renta
38

Karl Lagerfeld
40

Giorgio Armani
42

Azzedine Alaïa
44

Yves Saint Laurent
46

Issey Miyake
48

Kenzo Takada
50

Ralph Lauren
52

Roberto Cavalli
58

Vivienne Westwood
60

Rei Kawakubo
62

Calvin Klein
64

Yohji Yamamoto
66

Jil Sander
68

Paul Smith
70

ICONIC ITEMS

STATISTICS

Gianni Versace
72

Diane von Furstenberg
74

Donna Karan
76

Miuccia Prada
78

Franco Moschino
84

Tommy Hilfiger
86

Jean Paul Gaultier
88

Helmut Lang
90

Martin Margiela
92

Dries Van Noten
94

D. Dolce & S. Gabbana
96

Michael Kors
98

Ann Demeulemeester
100

John Galliano
106

Alber Elbaz
108

Tom Ford
110

Marc Jacobs
112

Thom Browne
114

Raf Simons
116

Hedi Slimane
118

Alexander McQueen
120

Hussein Chalayan
122

Nicolas Ghesquière
124

Stella McCartney
126

Riccardo Tisci
128

OTHERS

INTRODUCTION

Fashion design is about more than just clothes – there are stories behind every garment. These stories are driven by self-expression, cultural movements, political or social points of view, historical tributes, a simple desire to celebrate a certain piece of fabric, and so much more.

Some of the designers behind these stories have followed perfectly ordinary paths, enjoying successful careers and long, prosperous lives. Some have experienced lives full of tragedy, or cruel realities, and were taken from the world at the peak of their careers.

While there are plenty of incredibly talented designers around the world, this book focuses on 50 of the most recognized throughout history. You might learn things you didn't know when you first came across their designs. You might discover how they drew influence from other legends in this book. You might even find out that they're not at all who you thought they were.

We hope that by reading about each designer's unique journey, you will discover the moments that caused catalysts in their careers, and gain insight into their successes. We hope this book will fill you with the inspiration to forge your own unique path. One thing is for sure: after finishing this book, you will not view these fashion legends the same way again.

TIMELINES

Coco Chanel 1883
Cristóbal Balenciaga 1895
Christian Dior 1905
Pierre Balmain 1914
Emilio Pucci 1914
Pierre Cardin 1922
Hubert de Givenchy 1927
Mary Quant 1930
Sonia Rykiel 1930
Valentino Garavani 1932
Oscar de la Renta 1932
Karl Lagerfeld 1933
Giorgio Armani 1934
Azzedine Alaïa 1935
Yves Saint Laurent 1936
Issey Miyake 1938
Kenzo Takada 1939
Ralph Lauren 1939
Roberto Cavalli 1940
Vivienne Westwood 1941
Rei Kawakubo 1942
Calvin Klein 1942
Yohji Yamamoto 1943
Jil Sander 1943
Paul Smith 1946
Gianni Versace 1946
Diane von Furstenberg 1946
Donna Karan 1948
Miuccia Prada 1949
Franco Moschino 1950
Tommy Hilfiger 1951
Jean Paul Gaultier 1952
Helmut Lang
Martin Margiela
Dries Van Noten
Domenico Dolce & Stefano Gabbana
Michael Kors
Ann Demeulemeester
John Galliano
Alber Elbaz
Tom Ford
Marc Jacobs
Thom Browne
Raf Simons
Hedi Slimane
Alexander McQueen
Hussein Chalayan
Nicolas Ghesquière
Stella McCartney
Riccardo Tisci

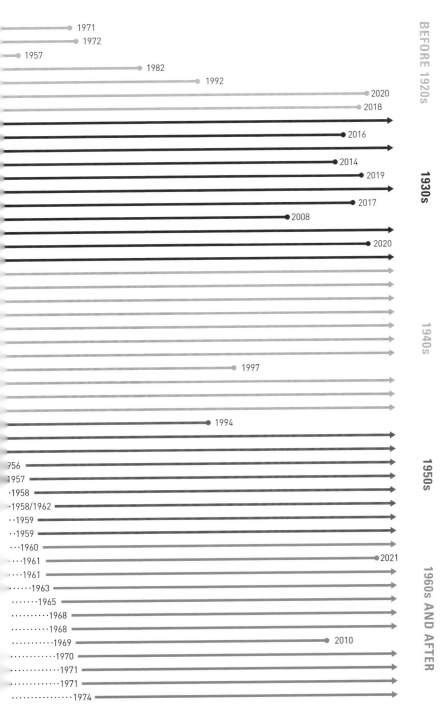

1971
1972
1957
1982
1992
2020
2018

2016
2014
2019
2017
2008
2020

1997

1994

956
957
1958
1958/1962
1959
1959
1960
1961
1961
1963
1965
1968
1968
1969
1970
1971
1971
1974

2021

2010

BORN BEFORE OR DURING THE

1920s

Designers born before and during the 1920s were significantly impacted by WWII. In a celebration of freedom, there was a new fashion direction: revolutionary silhouettes grew in popularity, providing excitement to consumers craving novelty and liberal designs, while rebelling against the dreary, boring uniforms of the war. It was also during this time that ready-to-wear collections began to rise, with Paris positioned as the arbiter of high fashion.

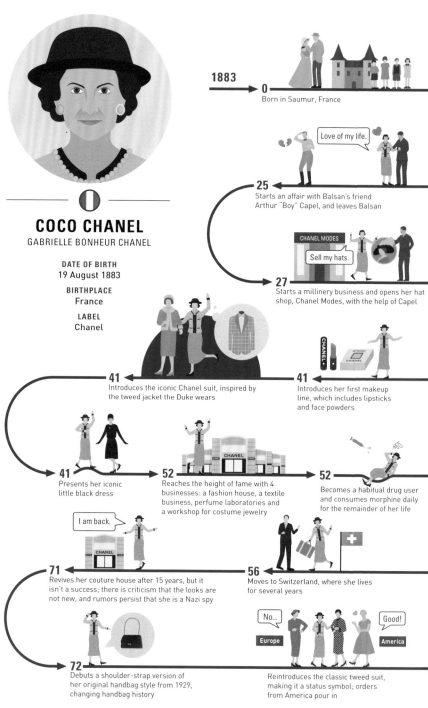

1883

0 — Born in Saumur, France

Love of my life.

25 — Starts an affair with Balsan's friend Arthur "Boy" Capel, and leaves Balsan

CHANEL MODES

Sell my hats.

27 — Starts a millinery business and opens her hat shop, Chanel Modes, with the help of Capel

CHANEL

41 — Introduces her first makeup line, which includes lipsticks and face powders

41 — Introduces the iconic Chanel suit, inspired by the tweed jacket the Duke wears

41 — Presents her iconic little black dress

CHANEL

52 — Reaches the height of fame with 4 businesses: a fashion house, a textile business, perfume laboratories and a workshop for costume jewelry

52 — Becomes a habitual drug user and consumes morphine daily for the remainder of her life

I am back.

CHANEL

71 — Revives her couture house after 15 years, but it isn't a success; there is criticism that the looks are not new, and rumors persist that she is a Nazi spy

56 — Moves to Switzerland, where she lives for several years

72 — Debuts a shoulder-strap version of her original handbag style from 1929, changing handbag history

No... Europe

Good! America

Reintroduces the classic tweed suit, making it a status symbol; orders from America pour in

COCO CHANEL
GABRIELLE BONHEUR CHANEL

DATE OF BIRTH
19 August 1883

BIRTHPLACE
France

LABEL
Chanel

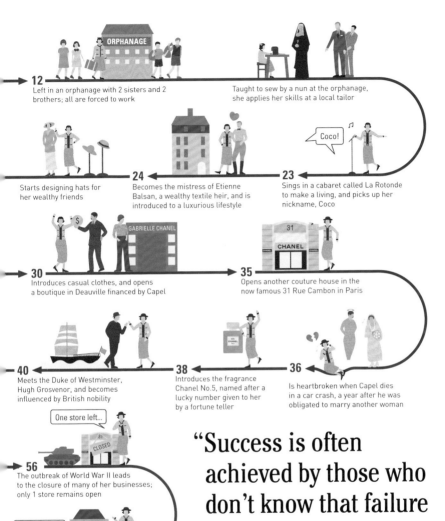

12 Left in an orphanage with 2 sisters and 2 brothers; all are forced to work

Taught to sew by a nun at the orphanage, she applies her skills at a local tailor

Coco!

23 Sings in a cabaret called La Rotonde to make a living, and picks up her nickname, Coco

24 Becomes the mistress of Etienne Balsan, a wealthy textile heir, and is introduced to a luxurious lifestyle

Starts designing hats for her wealthy friends

GABRIELLE CHANEL

30 Introduces casual clothes, and opens a boutique in Deauville financed by Capel

35 Opens another couture house in the now famous 31 Rue Cambon in Paris

40 Meets the Duke of Westminster, Hugh Grosvenor, and becomes influenced by British nobility

38 Introduces the fragrance Chanel No.5, named after a lucky number given to her by a fortune teller

36 Is heartbroken when Capel dies in a car crash, a year after he was obligated to marry another woman

One store left...

CLOSED

56 The outbreak of World War II leads to the closure of many of her businesses; only 1 store remains open

Is she a spy?...

RITZ HOTEL

Starts living at The Ritz, where she will remain for the rest of her life. Rumors persist that she is a Nazi spy, as the hotel is favored by Germans during the war

COCO CHANEL

88 Dies in her hotel room at The Ritz in Paris

"Success is often achieved by those who don't know that failure is inevitable."

CAREER HIGHLIGHTS

With a confidence that some considered arrogance, Coco Chanel was quite a rebel. Creating a niche early in her career with both her hats and her clothing, Chanel was able to work her way up from a poor, underprivileged youth to one of the most important fashion designers in history. Part of her success can be attributed to her ability to make the most out of every available opportunity and connection.

CRISTÓBAL BALENCIAGA

CRISTÓBAL BALENCIAGA EIZAGUIRRE

DATE OF BIRTH
21 January 1895

BIRTHPLACE
Spain

LABEL
Balenciaga

"A couturier must be an architect for design, a sculptor for shape, a painter for color, a musician for harmony, and a philosopher for temperance."

1895

0
Born to a seamstress in a small fishing village in Getaria, Spain

20
Opens his first shop, in San Sebastiàn; it is called Eisa, a short version of his mother's maiden name, Eizaguirre

20
Deconstructs couture dresses to study the tailoring skills of others

52
Presents the fragrance Le Dix, naming it after the street number of his atelier in Paris

52
Transforms silhouettes and presents his Barrel Line dress – a stark contrast to Christian Dior's New Look, which is trending at the time

53
Is devastated when his lover, Wladzio d'Attainville, dies; he considers closing the business and showcasing all-black dresses

65
Designs the wedding dress of the Queen of Belgium

72
Presents the dramatic Envelope Dress; although it's a hit with the press, only 2 are sold

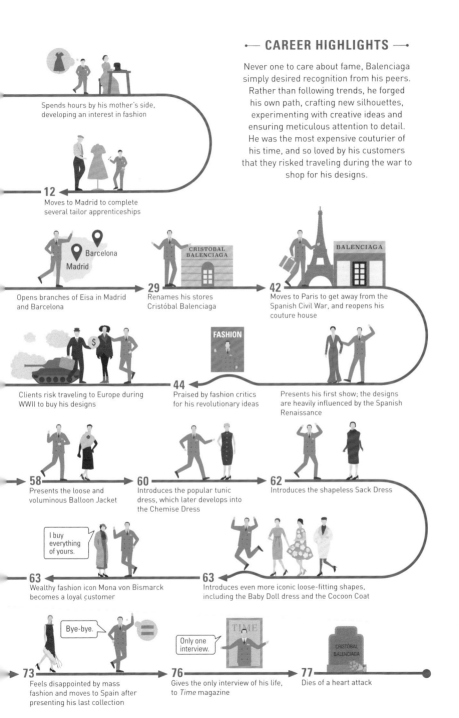

Spends hours by his mother's side, developing an interest in fashion

12
Moves to Madrid to complete several tailor apprenticeships

— CAREER HIGHLIGHTS —

Never one to care about fame, Balenciaga simply desired recognition from his peers. Rather than following trends, he forged his own path, crafting new silhouettes, experimenting with creative ideas and ensuring meticulous attention to detail. He was the most expensive couturier of his time, and so loved by his customers that they risked traveling during the war to shop for his designs.

Barcelona
Madrid
Opens branches of Eisa in Madrid and Barcelona

29
CRISTÓBAL BALENCIAGA
Renames his stores Cristóbal Balenciaga

42
BALENCIAGA
Moves to Paris to get away from the Spanish Civil War, and reopens his couture house

$
Clients risk traveling to Europe during WWII to buy his designs

FASHION

44
Praised by fashion critics for his revolutionary ideas

Presents his first show; the designs are heavily influenced by the Spanish Renaissance

58
Presents the loose and voluminous Balloon Jacket

60
Introduces the popular tunic dress, which later develops into the Chemise Dress

62
Introduces the shapeless Sack Dress

I buy everything of yours.

63
Wealthy fashion icon Mona von Bismarck becomes a loyal customer

63
Introduces even more iconic loose-fitting shapes, including the Baby Doll dress and the Cocoon Coat

Bye-bye.

73
Feels disappointed by mass fashion and moves to Spain after presenting his last collection

Only one interview.
TIME

76
Gives the only interview of his life, to *Time* magazine

CRISTÓBAL BALENCIAGA

77
Dies of a heart attack

CHRISTIAN DIOR

DATE OF BIRTH
21 January 1905

BIRTHPLACE
France

LABEL
Christian Dior

— **CAREER HIGHLIGHTS** —

With women growing tired of the masculine clothing styles that reigned supreme during the war years, Dior's New Look provided a welcome breath of fresh air and femininity. In part, it was Dior's perfect timing that contributed to his success, along with his strong sense of innovation and pioneering spirit.

1905

0

Born into a wealthy family in a seaside town in Normandy, France

30

Starts selling sketches of dresses and hats while living in a friend's attic

33

Works for fashion designer Robert Piguet

A way to preserve the fashion industry!

37

Dresses the wives of Nazi officers and French collaborators

Design for me?

No.

41

Rejects the invitation of textile magnate Marcel Boussac to resurrect Philippe et Gaston

Christian Dior
PARFUMS

43

Launches Dior Parfums, with Miss Dior being the first fragrance

New star of Parisian haute couture

Becomes the new star of the Parisian haute couture scene, oozing opulence as rationing and the war become a distant memory

44

Becomes the first couturier to introduce licensing for products including furs, socks, ties and perfumes

PARIS FASHION

$

72%
Christian Dior

Accounts for 72% of Paris fashion exports and 5% of France's total exports

20
Sells his fashion sketches to make pocket money

Political Science.

23
Feeling pressured by his father, he studies political science at the École des Sciences

GALLERY

CLOSED

29
Mourns the death of his mother, while his father's business collapses

GALLERY

26
Opens a small art gallery backed by his father, and is among the first to exhibit surrealist paintings

34
Called upon to serve in the military for 2 years

"By being natural and sincere, one often can create revolutions without having sought them."

LUCIEN LELONG

Joins the fashion house of Lucien Lelong, as primary designer, along with Pierre Balmain

Founds the house of Christian Dior with the support of Boussac

It's such a new look!

42
Presents his Corolle and En Huit lines, with *Harper's Bazaar* editor-in-chief Carmel Snow exclaiming, "It's such a new look!"

Lace-up corsets and long skirts again? No!

Protests against the New Look begin, with feminists becoming angry that women's newfound independence is being compromised

Rationing? But they use so much fabric!

King George V forbids Princess Elizabeth and Princess Margaret from wearing the New Look, which uses a lot of fabric

Je Suis Couturier.

46
Releases his first book, "Je Suis Couturier"

TIME

52
Becomes the first designer to be featured on the cover of *Time* magazine

CHRISTIAN DIOR

52
Dies of a heart attack during a spa vacation in Italy

PIERRE BALMAIN
PIERRE ALEXANDRE CLAUDIUS BALMAIN

DATE OF BIRTH
18 May 1914

BIRTHPLACE
France

LABEL
Balmain

"Keep to the basic principles of fashion and you will always be in harmony with the latest trends, without falling prey to them."

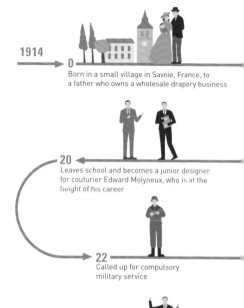

1914

0
Born in a small village in Savoie, France, to a father who owns a wholesale drapery business

20
Leaves school and becomes a junior designer for couturier Edward Molyneux, who is at the height of his career

22
Called up for compulsory military service

AUSTRALIA

33
Starts actively promoting himself internationally, and tours Australia

Launches Vent Vert, the first-ever green-floral fragrance; it becomes a bestseller in the late 1940s

REVLON $

Sells the Balmain perfume business to Revlon

40
Spots Karl Lagerfeld while judging a fashion competition, and hires him

Come help me.

Is chosen to design the wardrobe of Queen Sirikit of Thailand for an American tour

50
Writes his autobiography, "My Years and Seasons"

7
His father dies, leaving behind only a chest full of theatrical costumes

19
Studies architecture at the École des Beaux-Arts while freelancing for designer Robert Piguet as a sketch artist

LUCIEN LELONG

25
Completes his military service and joins couturier Lucien Lelong's team, working alongside Christian Dior

BALMAIN
PARIS

31
Establishes the house of Balmain, displaying bell-shaped, cinched-waist skirts

Balmain lacked support from his family to pursue his dreams, but he persisted and went on to become one of the best tailors of the century. He applied his talent to everything from simple tailored suits to extravagant evening gowns. Credited as being one of the leaders of the New Look generation, along with Christian Dior and Jacques Fath, Balmain's elegant, glamorous designs were favored by Hollywood stars and fashion icons including Katharine Hepburn and Vivien Leigh.

Bestselling garment!

29
Designs a black crepe afternoon dress for Lelong called Little Profit; it becomes a bestseller

Let's be partners?   No.

Suggests a partnership with Dior, but is turned down

34
Meets his partner, Danish designer Erik Mortensen, who will work at Balmain until 1991

AMERICA

Starts designing film costumes and off-screen clothes for Hollywood stars

37
Opens branches in the United States that sell his ready-to-wear collections

54
Creates outfits for the Grenoble Winter Olympics

AIRFRANCE

61
Designs the uniform for Air France's first female pilot

PIERRE BALMAIN

68
Dies of liver cancer in a hospital in Paris after completing the sketches for his next collection

EMILIO PUCCI

DATE OF BIRTH
20 November 1914

BIRTHPLACE
Italy

LABEL
Emilio Pucci

● CAREER HIGHLIGHTS ●

An innovator of bright, playful, swirling patterns and fluid fabrics, Emilio Pucci was a pioneer of resort wear, making casual, colorful clothing a desirable and internationally recognized style. Appropriately nicknamed "the Lord of Bright Colors" and "the King of Casual Couture", Pucci left a unique mark on the fashion world.

1914

0
Born into a noble Florentine family in Naples, Italy

33
Creates a ski outfit comprising a parka and tapered ski pants; it is photographed by *Harper's Bazaar's* Toni Frissell

35
Launches a swimwear line, but it doesn't sell well, so he moves into other categories

36
Opens his first boutique, in Capri

Sportswear chic.

37
Presents his first full collection with a new style called Sportswear Chic at the Palazzo Pitti

AMERICA

Becomes the first Italian designer to achieve big commercial success in the United States

46
Fashion icons including Sophia Loren, Jackie Kennedy and Marilyn Monroe are spotted wearing Pucci designs

I'm in the Liberal Party.

51
Serves as a member of Italian Parliament, representing the Liberal Party for 9 years

57
Designs full collections of uniforms for Texas-based airline Braniff International for 12 years

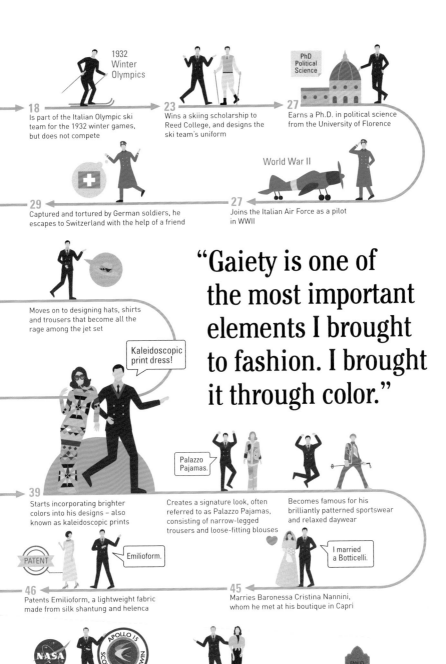

18 — Is part of the Italian Olympic ski team for the 1932 winter games, but does not compete

1932 Winter Olympics

23 — Wins a skiing scholarship to Reed College, and designs the ski team's uniform

27 — Earns a Ph.D. in political science from the University of Florence

PhD Political Science

29 — Captured and tortured by German soldiers, he escapes to Switzerland with the help of a friend

27 — Joins the Italian Air Force as a pilot in WWII

World War II

Moves on to designing hats, shirts and trousers that become all the rage among the jet set

Kaleidoscopic print dress!

"Gaiety is one of the most important elements I brought to fashion. I brought it through color."

39 — Starts incorporating brighter colors into his designs – also known as kaleidoscopic prints

Palazzo Pajamas.

Creates a signature look, often referred to as Palazzo Pajamas, consisting of narrow-legged trousers and loose-fitting blouses

Becomes famous for his brilliantly patterned sportswear and relaxed daywear

Emilioform.

I married a Botticelli.

46 — Patents Emilioform, a lightweight fabric made from silk shantung and helenca

45 — Marries Baronessa Cristina Nannini, whom he met at his boutique in Capri

76 — Creates the logo for Apollo 15

77 — Retires, with daughter Laudomia taking over the business

78 — Dies of a heart attack in a nursing home in Florence

PIERRE CARDIN
PIETRO CARDIN

DATE OF BIRTH
2 July 1922

BIRTHPLACE
Italy

LABELS
Christian Dior, Pierre Cardin

•── CAREER HIGHLIGHTS ──•

While he was never one to stick to a traditional business model, Cardin found ways to create a lucrative fashion business, becoming one of the wealthiest and most influential designers of the 1960s. A pioneering force, he was the first Western couturier to seek out Eastern influences, and the first to present a ready-to-wear collection. His Space Age-inspired collections are still influential.

1922 → **0**
Born in Italy to wealthy wine-merchant parents

24
Works in Dior's newly opened fashion house as the master tailor, and is in charge of the famous New Look collection

28
Launches his own company; Dior sends Cardin his overflow customers

This is not haute couture.

37
Presents his first ready-to-wear collection, which leads to his expulsion from the Chambre Syndicale; he is later reinstated

46
Fascinated by space, he presents futuristic collections, helping launch the Space Age look

Signs first-ever licensing contract outside of fashion, creating porcelain tableware

For theater, dance, music, painting and gastronomy.

ESPACE
pierre cardin

48
Buys the Théâtre des Ambassadeurs, turning it into a performance hall called Espace Pierre Cardin, which remains open until 2016

57
Designs the interior and exterior of an exclusive West Wind jet

2 Moves to France with his family and grows up in Saint-Étienne

8 Designs dresses for the dolls of his neighbor's child

14 Works as an apprentice at a tailoring house

24 Designs costumes for Jean Cocteau and Christian Bérard's film "Beauty and the Beast"

23 Starts working for leading French designers Jeanne Paquin and Elsa Schiaparelli

22 Accepts a job with the French Red Cross that takes him to Paris

Designs suits, gradually gaining a solid reputation for his skills

31 Shows his first haute couture collection and becomes a member of the Chambre Syndicale

My famous three-dimensional cut.

JAPAN

35 Seeks influence in Japan, and gives lessons on his famous 3D cut as an honorary professor at the Bunka Fashion College

ASIA

Becomes one of the first fashion houses to expand into Asia – first in Japan, and 22 years later in China

32 Presents his famous Bubble Dress

38 Launches his first men's collection and creates a men's ready-to-wear department

44 Gathers all the triplets he can find in Paris to model in his first children's collection

> "The dress is a vase which the body follows. My clothes are like modules in which bodies move."

Festival de Lacoste

79 Buys the Marquis de Sade's castle and creates the annual Lacoste Festival

pierre cardin

84 Opens his museum, Past-Present-Future, in Saint-Ouen; it later moves to central Paris

PIERRE CARDIN

98 Dies at the American Hospital of Paris

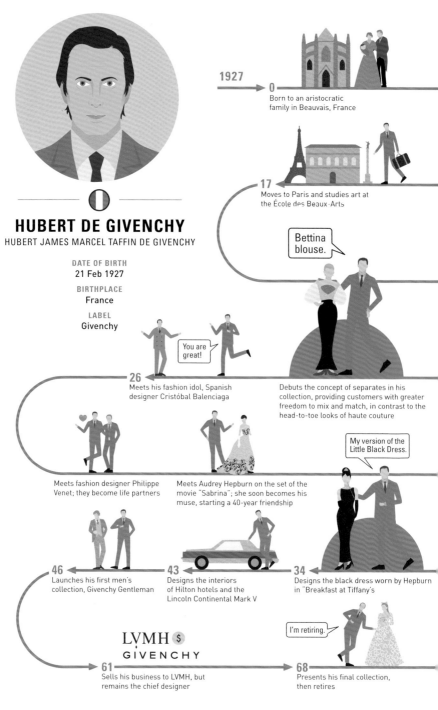

HUBERT DE GIVENCHY
HUBERT JAMES MARCEL TAFFIN DE GIVENCHY

DATE OF BIRTH
21 Feb 1927

BIRTHPLACE
France

LABEL
Givenchy

1927

0
Born to an aristocratic family in Beauvais, France

17
Moves to Paris and studies art at the École des Beaux-Arts

Bettina blouse.

You are great!

26
Meets his fashion idol, Spanish designer Cristóbal Balenciaga

Debuts the concept of separates in his collection, providing customers with greater freedom to mix and match, in contrast to the head-to-toe looks of haute couture

My version of the Little Black Dress.

Meets fashion designer Philippe Venet; they become life partners

Meets Audrey Hepburn on the set of the movie "Sabrina"; she soon becomes his muse, starting a 40-year friendship

46
Launches his first men's collection, Givenchy Gentleman

43
Designs the interiors of Hilton hotels and the Lincoln Continental Mark V

34
Designs the black dress worn by Hepburn in "Breakfast at Tiffany's

LVMH $

GIVENCHY

I'm retiring.

61
Sells his business to LVMH, but remains the chief designer

68
Presents his final collection, then retires

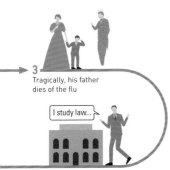

3
Tragically, his father dies of the flu

I study law...

Urged by his mother, he studies law at university

> "To have style is to have a feeling for what is currently fashionable, and still to simultaneously remain true to oneself."

CAREER HIGHLIGHTS

Givenchy gained immediate success after introducing the concept of separates in his debut collection. His winning streak continued with his simple, elegant designs that women loved to wear. One of those women was actress Audrey Hepburn, who built a lifelong friendship with the designer. While Chanel invented the Little Black Dress, it was Hepburn and Givenchy who made the style hugely popular.

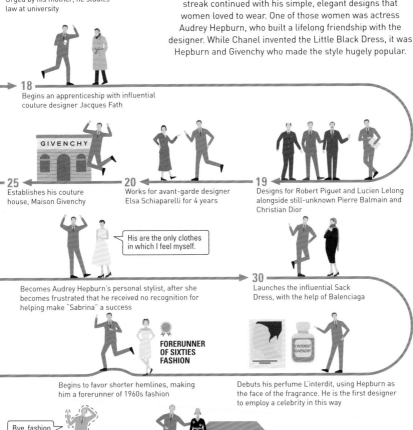

18
Begins an apprenticeship with influential couture designer Jacques Fath

GIVENCHY

25
Establishes his couture house, Maison Givenchy

20
Works for avant-garde designer Elsa Schiaparelli for 4 years

19
Designs for Robert Piguet and Lucien Lelong alongside still-unknown Pierre Balmain and Christian Dior

His are the only clothes in which I feel myself.

Becomes Audrey Hepburn's personal stylist, after she becomes frustrated that he received no recognition for helping make "Sabrina" a success

30
Launches the influential Sack Dress, with the help of Balenciaga

FORERUNNER OF SIXTIES FASHION

Begins to favor shorter hemlines, making him a forerunner of 1960s fashion

L'INTERDIT GIVENCHY

Debuts his perfume L'interdit, using Hepburn as the face of the fragrance. He is the first designer to employ a celebrity in this way

Bye, fashion world.

HUBERT DE GIVENCHY

83
Removes himself from the fashion world, rarely making public appearances

90
Curates a self-titled exhibition at the Museum of Lace and Fashion in Calais, France

91
Dies in his sleep at his home on the outskirts of Paris

ICONIC ITEMS

BY DESIGNERS BORN BEFORE OR DURING THE 1920s

1

2.55 FLAP BAG – COCO CHANEL

Introduced in 1955
Tired of carrying handbags, Chanel made it acceptable, and fashionable, for women with considerable social status to carry a bag on their shoulder by adding thin straps – inspired by soldiers' bags – to her purse designs. Karl Lagerfeld later made the style one of the most sought-after handbags in history.

2

NEW LOOK – CHRISTIAN DIOR

Introduced in 1947
Two years after WWII, Dior offered a stark contrast to the gloomy uniform of the war by presenting his New Look. The revolutionary silhouette emphasized the proportions of a woman and sparked a significant shift in post-war fashion.

3

BARREL LINE DRESS – CRISTÓBAL BALENCIAGA

Introduced in 1947
Balenciaga offered women an alternative silhouette to Dior's New Look with his Barrel Line dress, which broadens the wearer's shoulders and de-emphasizes the waist. The style offered women a fresh way of dressing.

4 KALEIDOSCOPIC PRINTS – EMILIO PUCCI

Introduced in 1953
Inspired by the colors, cultures and natural landscapes of the Mediterranean, Pucci presented kaleidoscopic prints that mimicked contemporary art forms. It was the first time such optical illusions had been incorporated into clothing.

5 LITTLE BLACK DRESS – HUBERT DE GIVENCHY

Introduced in 1961
Givenchy designed a black sheath dress for his muse and close friend Audrey Hepburn to wear in the opening scene of the romantic comedy film "Breakfast at Tiffany's". One of the world's most famous dresses, it sold for a historic price of more than US$900,000 at Christie's in London in 2006.

6 SPACE AGE – PIERRE CARDIN

Introduced in 1968
Cardin explored the idea of futuristic styles when space travel became popular on TV in the 1960s. His fashion-forward astronaut look – a vision shared by André Courrèges and Paco Rabanne – took off long before humans landed on the moon, and has been imitated all over the world.

1930s

The brutality of the war continued to leave young people, as well as many designers, avoiding the tide of postwar business and conformity. Instead, a casual, non-conformist approach to fashion began to brew – one that stressed individuality. Designers began drawing influence from youth culture, including pop music and the hippie movement. It was also during this era that a number of designers from the US and Japan began to contribute to the fashion world.

MARY QUANT
BARBARA MARY QUANT

DATE OF BIRTH
11 February 1930

BIRTHPLACE
United Kingdom

LABEL
Mary Quant

"Rules are invented for lazy people who don't want to think for themselves."

1930

0
Born in the Blackheath area of southeast London

It is exhausting, but my rail is refreshed!

Adopts a hand-to-mouth production cycle, paying for materials for the next day's stock with the sales from the current day, and sewing garments overnight

Loud music, free drinks, witty window displays.

Attracts a large number of young women to her boutique, Bazaar. They're searching for youthful luxury designs, which are difficult to find at other high-end shops

Mary Quant Ginger Group

29
Expands into the UK mass market with a new, cheaper diffusion line, Ginger Group

Becomes the first designer to use PVC, creating "wet-look" clothes

'Colour by Quant' and 'Quant on Make-up.'

Designs and launches a cosmetics line, Mary Quant Cosmetics

Quant by Quant

32
Publishes an autobiography called "Quant by Quant", the first of many books

Experiences a rise in popularity spurred by the influence of the era's most high-profile model, Twiggy

54
Designs the interior of a special-edition Mini Cooper

MARY QUANT COLOUR

60
Opens Mary Quant Colour, the brand's first cosmetics shop, in London

I study illustration!

16

Studies illustration at London's Goldsmiths College

Starts an apprenticeship at Erik, a high-end Mayfair milliner, while struggling to make ends meet

21

Opens a shop with former classmate Alexander Plunket Greene and lawyer-turned-photographer Archie McNair

I'm a trendsetter.

I like your short skirts.

Inspires her customers with what she wears, and introduces them to some of her bestselling styles

23

Marries Plunket Greene and starts designing her own clothing line, with no formal education

— CAREER HIGHLIGHTS —

Quant started a fashion revolution during the 1960s, launching the miniskirt and popularizing the "mod" movement. A significant figure in London's youth fashion scene, Quant built a brand with a commercial mindset, distributing her creations globally and not limiting herself to fashion. She produced everything from cosmetics to carpets and toys. Her colorful, quirky designs encouraged consumers to express themselves rather than conform to societal norms.

Customers demand even shorter skirts, spurring Quant to pioneer the miniskirt trend

28

Enters the American market by signing a licensing agreement with J.C. Penney for clothing and underwear

Popularizes hot pants and revolutionizes the way women dress

$7 MILLION

35

The amount of Quant's garments being found in women's wardrobes rises to an estimated US$7 million

38

Starts designing ties – her first menswear product

52

The designer's first beauty book, "Quant on Make-up", is published in the UK to great success

42

Works on the advisory council of the Victoria and Albert Museum for 2 years

39

Holds a retrospective exhibition, "Mary Quant's London", at the London Museum

66

Resigns as director of Mary Quant Ltd., her cosmetics company, after a Japanese buyout

81

Appointed Dame Commander of the Order of the British Empire and receives honors for her service to British fashion

SONIA RYKIEL
SONIA FLIS

DATE OF BIRTH
25 May 1930

BIRTHPLACE
France

LABEL
Sonia Rykiel

1930

0

Born in Neuilly, just west of Paris, to a Russian mother and a Romanian watchmaker father; she is the eldest of 5 sisters

23

Marries Sam Rykiel, owner of a boutique called Laura that sells elegant clothing

32

I will make my own sweater!

When she struggles to find a sweater to wear during pregnancy, she designs her own using a Venice supplier used by husband

FRENCH FEDERATION OF FASHION
Vice-President

43
Elected vice-president of French fashion's governing body, the French Federation of Fashion, Ready-to-Wear Couturiers, and Fashion Designers

45

Her daughter, Nathalie, joins the label as a model; she later becomes vice-president and art director

47

Designs 3 looks for mail-order firm 3 Suisses; becomes one of the first designers to initiate mass-market distribution

Groups!

Starts sending models out in groups, and is credited with making runway shows fun again

77

President of Sonia Rykiel!

Appoints Nathalie president of Sonia Rykiel

72

RYKIEL Woman

Launches Rykiel Woman, a lingerie and erotica shop that sells sex toys

78

Tributes are paid to Rykiel by 30 fashion designers in celebration of the brand's 40th anniversary

Stages an exhibition of her designs at the Musée des Arts Décoratifs in Paris from 2008 to 2009

79

Collaborates with H&M on Sonia Rykiel Pour H&M

17
Works in a Parisian textile store, Grande Maison de Blanc, doing window displays

"The arrangement is amazing!"

She is complimented by Henri Matisse on her arrangement of colorful scarves; the French artist buys every style

— CAREER HIGHLIGHTS —

Crowned "the Queen of Knits" by *Women's Wear Daily*, Rykiel has been an iconic figure since the 1960s. She came out with a signature range of colorful sweaters that were perfectly timed with the Swinging London era, during which pop art and music greatly energized young people. As well as adopting pioneering fashion techniques, Rykiel was the first to use slogans on sweaters.

"Poor Boy sweater!"

33
Sells her first shrunken sweater, the Poor Boy sweater, in her husband's shop

The sweater makes the cover of *Elle* magazine, and Audrey Hepburn buys it in 14 colors

SONIA RYKIEL

35
Launches the Sonia Rykiel brand, with the help of her husband

41
One of the first designers to feature slogans on her clothing, including the word "sensuous"; the style becomes a bestseller

38
Files for divorce from Sam Rykiel

QUEEN OF KNITS

37
Crowned "the Queen of Knits" by *Women's Wear Daily*

SONIA BY SONIA RYKIEL

59
Launches a more affordable ready-to-wear line, later renamed Sonia by Sonia Rykiel. It closes in 2013

PARIS

65
Collaborates with music impresario Malcolm McLaren on his song "Who the Hell Is Sonia Rykiel?"

"I have the feeling I've always done what I wanted throughout my life."

82
Becomes majority-owned by Hong Kong-based First Heritage Brands, part of the investment company Fung Brands Limited

Reveals that she has been suffering from Parkinson's disease for 15 years

86
Dies of a complication from Parkinson's at her home in Paris

VALENTINO GARAVANI
VALENTINO CLEMENTE LUDOVICO GARAVANI

DATE OF BIRTH
11 May 1932

BIRTHPLACE
Italy

LABEL
Valentino

"Elegance is the balance between proportion, emotion and surprise."

⸻ CAREER HIGHLIGHTS ⸻

While finance and business were never Garavani's strong suits (his father helped fund the business in the early stages, and his business partner kept it from going bankrupt), his gowns are some of the most magnificent in fashion. The epitome of luxury and elegance, his intricate eveningwear creations – along with his trademark Valentino Red – form the pillars of his collections. His love of luxury runs through not just his designs, but also his personal life, which earned him the fond nickname "the King of High Living".

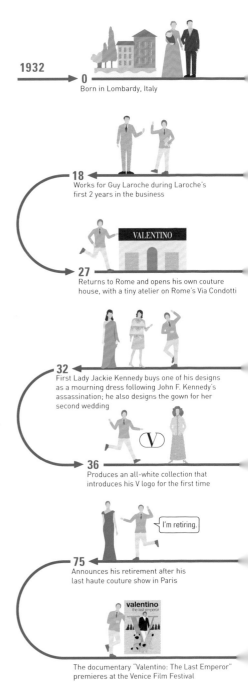

1932
0
Born in Lombardy, Italy

18
Works for Guy Laroche during Laroche's first 2 years in the business

27
Returns to Rome and opens his own couture house, with a tiny atelier on Rome's Via Condotti

32
First Lady Jackie Kennedy buys one of his designs as a mourning dress following John F. Kennedy's assassination; he also designs the gown for her second wedding

36
Produces an all-white collection that introduces his V logo for the first time

I'm retiring.

75
Announces his retirement after his last haute couture show in Paris

The documentary "Valentino: The Last Emperor" premieres at the Venice Film Festival

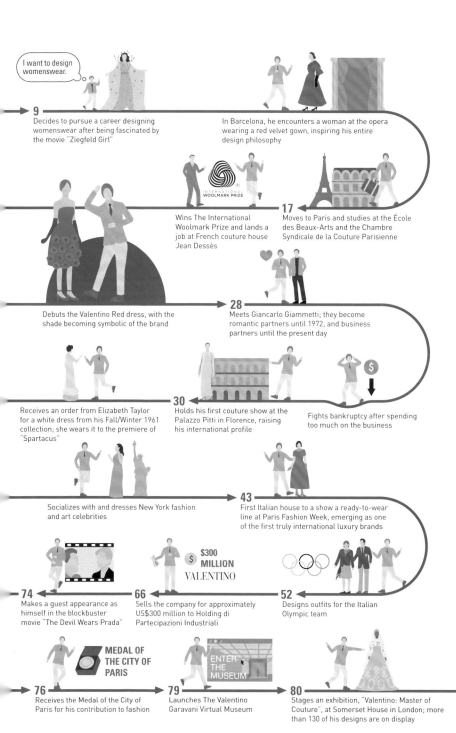

I want to design womenswear.

9
Decides to pursue a career designing womenswear after being fascinated by the movie "Ziegfeld Girl"

In Barcelona, he encounters a woman at the opera wearing a red velvet gown, inspiring his entire design philosophy

Wins The International Woolmark Prize and lands a job at French couture house Jean Dessès

17
Moves to Paris and studies at the École des Beaux-Arts and the Chambre Syndicale de la Couture Parisienne

Debuts the Valentino Red dress, with the shade becoming symbolic of the brand

28
Meets Giancarlo Giammetti; they become romantic partners until 1972, and business partners until the present day

Receives an order from Elizabeth Taylor for a white dress from his Fall/Winter 1961 collection; she wears it to the premiere of "Spartacus"

30
Holds his first couture show at the Palazzo Pitti in Florence, raising his international profile

Fights bankruptcy after spending too much on the business

Socializes with and dresses New York fashion and art celebrities

43
First Italian house to a show a ready-to-wear line at Paris Fashion Week, emerging as one of the first truly international luxury brands

74
Makes a guest appearance as himself in the blockbuster movie "The Devil Wears Prada"

$300 MILLION
VALENTINO

66
Sells the company for approximately US$300 million to Holding di Partecipazioni Industriali

52
Designs outfits for the Italian Olympic team

MEDAL OF THE CITY OF PARIS

76
Receives the Medal of the City of Paris for his contribution to fashion

ENTER THE MUSEUM

79
Launches The Valentino Garavani Virtual Museum

80
Stages an exhibition, "Valentino: Master of Couture", at Somerset House in London; more than 130 of his designs are on display

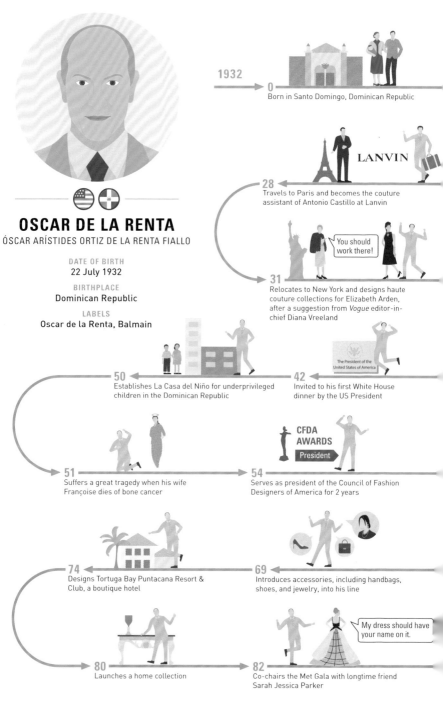

OSCAR DE LA RENTA
ÓSCAR ARÍSTIDES ORTIZ DE LA RENTA FIALLO

DATE OF BIRTH
22 July 1932

BIRTHPLACE
Dominican Republic

LABELS
Oscar de la Renta, Balmain

1932
0
Born in Santo Domingo, Dominican Republic

LANVIN
28
Travels to Paris and becomes the couture assistant of Antonio Castillo at Lanvin

You should work there!
31
Relocates to New York and designs haute couture collections for Elizabeth Arden, after a suggestion from *Vogue* editor-in-chief Diana Vreeland

The President of the United States of America
42
Invited to his first White House dinner by the US President

50
Establishes La Casa del Niño for underprivileged children in the Dominican Republic

51
Suffers a great tragedy when his wife Françoise dies of bone cancer

CFDA AWARDS
President
54
Serves as president of the Council of Fashion Designers of America for 2 years

74
Designs Tortuga Bay Puntacana Resort & Club, a boutique hotel

69
Introduces accessories, including handbags, shoes, and jewelry, into his line

80
Launches a home collection

My dress should have your name on it.
82
Co-chairs the Met Gala with longtime friend Sarah Jessica Parker

I want to be an abstract painter!

Interested in fashion...

19
Moves to Madrid and studies painting at the Real Academia de Bellas Artes de San Fernando

Develops an interests in fashion, and learns the basics of fabrics and fitting during his own suit-tailoring appointments

Creates his first dress for the daughter of a US ambassador, and lands on the cover of *Life* magazine

25
Earns a living as a fashion illustrator for magazines and Balenciaga

Oscar de la Renta

33
Becomes business partners with designer Jane Derby, but soon sets off on his own, launching his eponymous label

35
Marries French *Vogue* editor-in-chief Françoise de Langlade

COTY AWARDS

CFDA AWARDS
President

41
Serves as president of the Council of Fashion Designers of America for 3 years, and replaces the Coty Awards with the CFDA Awards

Dresses First Lady Jackie Kennedy, and becomes popular with many other first ladies

58
Marries American philanthropist Annette Engelhard Reed

PIERRE BALMAIN

60
Joins Pierre Balmain's team for the next 10 years, becoming the first American to head a French couture house

OSCAR DE LA RENTA

82
Passes away after a long battle with cancer

"Work hard. Believe in yourself. It's not the publicity that sells the clothes, it's the woman."

—————— CAREER HIGHLIGHTS ——————

De la Renta was fashion's favorite ladies' man. Good-looking and oozing charisma, the designer had a knack for knowing exactly what women wanted – and that included what they wanted to wear. His glamorous, feminine eye and impressive craftsmanship made for breathtaking collections adored by women around the world, including many American first ladies.

KARL LAGERFELD
KARL OTTO LAGERFELT

DATE OF BIRTH
10 September 1933

BIRTHPLACE
Germany

LABELS
Jean Patou, Chloé, Fendi, Chanel,
Karl Lagerfeld

— CAREER HIGHLIGHTS —

A man of many talents, Lagerfeld was a designer, artist, photographer, costume designer, weight-loss guru, and bookshop owner over the course of his successful career. The multitasker won his first fashion prize at just 21 years old, and remained one of the most powerful men in fashion until his death in 2019. Impressively balancing work for Chanel, Fendi and his own label along with other creative projects, Lagerfeld possessed the ability to make decisions swiftly while remaining confident in his choices.

1933

0
Born in Hamburg; his father is a wealthy businessman

Come help me.

21
Works as Pierre Balmain's assistant after winning in the coat category at the International Wool Secretariat Design Awards; Yves Saint Laurent wins in the dress category

Design Director

50
Invited by Chanel chairman Alain Wertheimer to become the house's design director

Reincarnates Chanel and captures a new generation of customers

74
Releases a documentary film, "Lagerfeld Confidential"

Sells some of his trademarks, including Lagerfeld Gallery, to Tommy Hilfiger, but maintains full design involvement

You can see it from space!

After 12 months of planning and preparation, stages the world's longest runway show, for Fendi, on the Great Wall of China

I want to marry her, but I can't.

78
Receives a cat, Choupette, as a gift from model Baptiste Giabiconi; he makes her a social media star

81
Transforms the Grand Palais into a Chanel supermarket for the AW14 show

Cartoonist · $$$ · Fashion designer

Aspires to be a cartoonist, but realizes fashion design could be more profitable

"I don't like standard beauty – there is no beauty without strangeness."

14
Moves to Paris and majors in drawing and history at Lycée Montaigne

JEAN PATOU
PARIS
Artistic Director

24
Works as artistic director for couturier Jean Patou for 5 years, but quickly feels bored

FASHION

The skirt is too short ...

25
Debuts his first collection, filled with very short skirts; it is poorly received

It sounds "more commercial".

LAGERFELD

29
Begins his freelance career and changes his surname from Lagerfelt to Lagerfeld

Has a relationship with socialite Jacques de Bascher, until Bascher's death in 1989

Use this logo!

32
Starts working for Fendi furs, and works on all ready-to-wear collections soon after

Chloé
Principal Designer

31
Takes a freelance role at Chloé and eventually becomes the principal designer for 15 years

KARL LAGERFELD
PARIS

51
Launches his own label, Karl Lagerfeld

Again.

Chloé

59
Returns to Chloé for another 5 years

DIESEL

65
Launches the Lagerfeld Gallery label, which later presents a denim collaboration with Diesel that sells 90% of its stock in the first week

H&M

71
Becomes the first designer to collaborate with H&M on an affordable collection

I want to wear Hedi's jeans.

THE KARL LAGERFELD DIET

68
Loses 42kg in 13 months and launches a diet book, "The Karl Lagerfeld Diet"

Many great art books.

7

66
Opens the Editions 7L publishing house and 7L bookshop, which is often used in his label's ad campaigns

84
Launches a rocket at the Grand Palais during the AW17 Chanel show

2017

Receives Paris' highest distinction, the Medal of the City of Paris, from the Mayor

KARL OTTO LAGERFELT

85
Dies in Paris from complications of pancreatic cancer. Choupette inherits his fortune

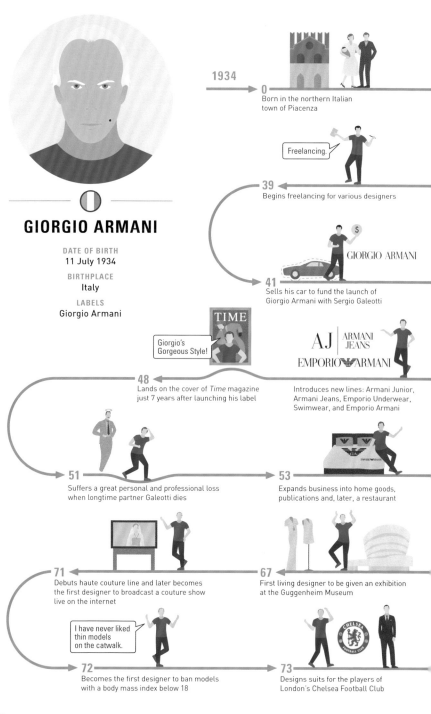

GIORGIO ARMANI

DATE OF BIRTH
11 July 1934

BIRTHPLACE
Italy

LABELS
Giorgio Armani

1934

0
Born in the northern Italian town of Piacenza

Freelancing.

39
Begins freelancing for various designers

41
Sells his car to fund the launch of Giorgio Armani with Sergio Galeotti

Giorgio's Gorgeous Style!

48
Lands on the cover of *Time* magazine just 7 years after launching his label

Introduces new lines: Armani Junior, Armani Jeans, Emporio Underwear, Swimwear, and Emporio Armani

51
Suffers a great personal and professional loss when longtime partner Galeotti dies

53
Expands business into home goods, publications and, later, a restaurant

71
Debuts haute couture line and later becomes the first designer to broadcast a couture show live on the internet

67
First living designer to be given an exhibition at the Guggenheim Museum

I have never liked thin models on the catwalk.

72
Becomes the first designer to ban models with a body mass index below 18

73
Designs suits for the players of London's Chelsea Football Club

Makes dolls out of mud, and hides a coffee bean inside each one

Department of Medicine.

UNIVERSITÀ CATTOLICA del Sacro Cuore

16
Enrolls in the Department of Medicine at the University of Piacenza

19
Leaves university and joins the army

Meets architectural craftsman Sergio Galeotti and develops a personal and professional relationship

30
Joins Nino Cerruti as a menswear designer

23
Finishes military service and works as a window dresser at La Rinascente for 7 years

Power Suit!

Presents the Power Suit, which becomes a symbol of success for many professionals

USA

45
Barneys New York airs a television commercial to introduce Armani to the United States, opening up the American market

American Gigolo

46
Designs clothing for the film "American Gigolo", starring Richard Gere, establishing himself in Hollywood

I was wrong.

TAX OFFICIALS

55
Receives suspended sentences and pays a fine for bribing tax officials in 1989 and 1990 for friendly tax audits

GIORGIO ARMANI beauty

62
Founds Giorgio Armani Beauty and creates cult-favorite makeup products

ARMANI Hotel Dubai

76
Opens his first hotel in Dubai's iconic skyscraper, Burj Khalifa

"Remain true to yourself and your philosophy."

—— **CAREER HIGHLIGHTS** ——

Armani – who did not debut his first collection until he was in his 40s – did everything in his career his way. Refusing to run with the pack, and instead forging his own path, has been a huge part of his success, and he has never strayed from his understated and elegant designs. He projected his own authority and self-confidence with the Power Suit, which was hugely successful in the 1980s.

AZZEDINE ALAÏA

DATE OF BIRTH
26 February 1935

BIRTHPLACE
Tunisia

LABELS
Alaïa

—— CAREER HIGHLIGHTS ——

Never one to follow the fashion week schedule or trends, Alaïa managed to maintain a strong identity throughout his decades as a designer. His personal style – he was fond of wearing simple black cotton Chinese pajamas – was in stark contrast to his creations, which, due to their figure-hugging silhouettes, earned him the nickname "the King of Cling." His warm, caring personality also helped him gain many celebrity friends, who treated him like family.

1935 · 0
Born in Tunis, Tunisia, into a wheat-farming family; he has a twin sister, Hafida

Becomes a dressmaker's assistant after graduating, copying couture gowns for wealthy Tunisian clients

22
Moves to Paris and works for Christian Dior, but has to leave after just 5 days due to a paperwork problem

Where is your coat from?

This is Alaïa.

A buyer for Bergdorf Goodman stops interior designer Andrée Putman on the street to ask where her coat is from; soon the store starts selling Alaïa

49
Creates clothing worn by Grace Jones in the Bond film "A View to a Kill"

Come live here.

69
Opens a 3-apartment hotel in Paris

Sells shares to the Prada Group, but maintains a level of independence

72
Buys back his brand and ready-to-wear collection, leaving Prada to control only his footwear division

76
Presents his first couture show in 7 years

Claims to have turned down the National Order of the Legion of Honor in 2008 – the highest civilian order in France

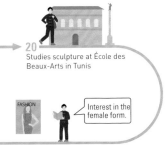

20 Studies sculpture at École des Beaux-Arts in Tunis

Interest in the female form.

Develops an interest in the female form while working as an assistant to a local midwife, Madame Pineau, who keeps fashion magazines in her clinic

"I am never sure that anything is good enough. Something that is good today will not be good tomorrow."

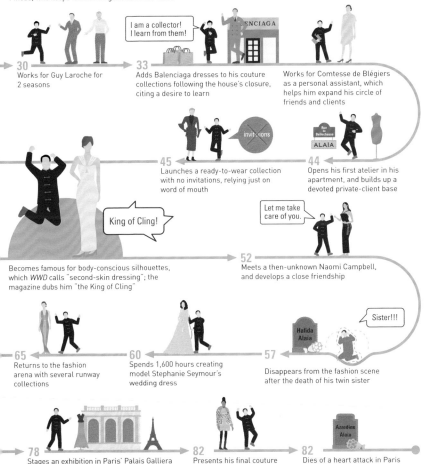

30 Works for Guy Laroche for 2 seasons

I am a collector! I learn from them!

33 Adds Balenciaga dresses to his couture collections following the house's closure, citing a desire to learn

Works for Comtesse de Blégiers as a personal assistant, which helps him expand his circle of friends and clients

45 Launches a ready-to-wear collection with no invitations, relying just on word of mouth

44 Opens his first atelier in his apartment, and builds up a devoted private-client base

King of Cling!

Becomes famous for body-conscious silhouettes, which WWD calls "second-skin dressing"; the magazine dubs him "the King of Cling"

Let me take care of you.

52 Meets a then-unknown Naomi Campbell, and develops a close friendship

Sister!!!

65 Returns to the fashion arena with several runway collections

60 Spends 1,600 hours creating model Stephanie Seymour's wedding dress

57 Disappears from the fashion scene after the death of his twin sister

78 Stages an exhibition in Paris' Palais Galliera

82 Presents his final couture show, his first in 6 years

82 Dies of a heart attack in Paris

YVES SAINT LAURENT

YVES HENRI DONAT MATHIEU-SAINT-LAURENT

DATE OF BIRTH
1 August 1936

BIRTHPLACE
Algeria

LABELS
**Christian Dior,
Yves Saint Laurent**

1936

I am a director of an insurance company.

0
Born in Oran, Algeria, to the director of an insurance company; he lives with his family by the sea

12
Presents his first fashion show, with his 2 sisters acting as clients

Published in *Vogue*!

17
Shows fashion sketches to Michel de Brunhoff, the editor of French *Vogue*, and immediately gets published

Experiencing hazing...

Christian Dior
Chief Designer

24
Is called up for military service in Algeria; he experiences hazing by his peers, resulting in admittance to a military hospital

21
Becomes chief designer after the death of Christian Dior, and meets Pierre Bergé, his partner for the rest of his life

Bye.

Chief Designer
Christian Dior

$140,000
Christian Dior

Returns to Paris and finds he has been replaced by Dior's former assistant, Marc Bohan

Obtains compensation from Dior for breaching his contract

47
Becomes the first living fashion designer to be honored by the Metropolitan Museum of Art with a solo exhibition

40
Breaks up with Bergé, but they remain business partners

COCAINE

Addiction to alcohol and cocaine increases

GUCCI
$ → YSL

63
Sells the house of Yves Saint Laurent to Gucci, and expresses displeasure when Tom Ford is named creative director

6
Bullied daily by schoolmates for appearing to be homosexual

Makes paper dolls and dresses them in swatches of fabric

Studies at the École de la Chambre Syndicale de la Couture Parisienne

"Fashion fades, style is eternal."

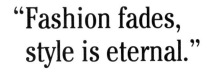

● ——— CAREER HIGHLIGHTS ———— ●

Being bullied at school rooted Saint Laurent's adolescent years in depression. He escaped into a fantasy world of fashion and, with support from industry leaders including Christian Dior, went on to become one of the most celebrated designers of the 20th century, presenting iconic designs including the Le Smoking suit and the Mondrian dress. Later in life, the vulnerable and suffering artist turned to alcohol and drug abuse, with depression taking over until his final days.

Becomes an assistant to Christian Dior through his connection to de Brunhoff

18
Wins first place in the dress category at the International Wool Secretariat Design Competition; Karl Lagerfeld wins the coat category

26
Opens his own fashion house with Pierre Bergé's help

29
Presents the now-famous Mondrian collection

How beautiful the color is!

30
Travels to Morocco for the first time, falling in love with the country

35
Causes a sensation by posing nude for the YSL Pour Homme cologne campaign

Publishes a cartoon story called "La Vilaine Lulu", mocking fashion society

Introduces the first female tuxedo, the iconic Le Smoking

66
Retires after his final haute couture show, and resides in Marrakech

71
Promoted to the rank of Grand Officer of the Legion of Honor, following his rank of Officer in 1985 and Commander in 2001

71
Dies of brain cancer at his Paris residence

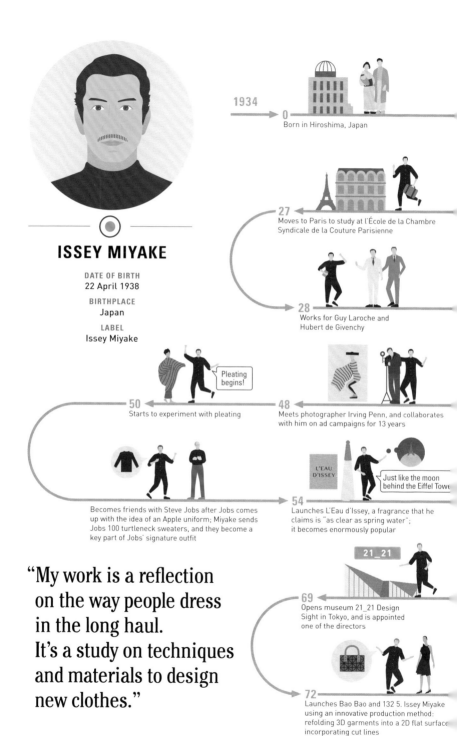

ISSEY MIYAKE

DATE OF BIRTH
22 April 1938

BIRTHPLACE
Japan

LABEL
Issey Miyake

1934
0
Born in Hiroshima, Japan

27
Moves to Paris to study at l'École de la Chambre Syndicale de la Couture Parisienne

28
Works for Guy Laroche and Hubert de Givenchy

Pleating begins!

50
Starts to experiment with pleating

48
Meets photographer Irving Penn, and collaborates with him on ad campaigns for 13 years

Becomes friends with Steve Jobs after Jobs comes up with the idea of an Apple uniform; Miyake sends Jobs 100 turtleneck sweaters, and they become a key part of Jobs' signature outfit

L'EAU D'ISSEY

Just like the moon behind the Eiffel Tower

54
Launches L'Eau d'Issey, a fragrance that he claims is "as clear as spring water"; it becomes enormously popular

21_21

69
Opens museum 21_21 Design Sight in Tokyo, and is appointed one of the directors

"My work is a reflection on the way people dress in the long haul. It's a study on techniques and materials to design new clothes."

72
Launches Bao Bao and 132 5. Issey Miyake using an innovative production method: refolding 3D garments into a 2D flat surface incorporating cut lines

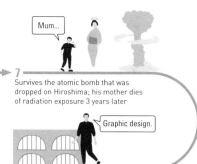

7

Survives the atomic bomb that was dropped on Hiroshima; his mother dies of radiation exposure 3 years later

26

Graduates from Tama Art University in Tokyo, where he studies graphic design

— **CAREER HIGHLIGHTS** —

Since the beginning of his career, forward-thinking designer Miyake had a passion for experimenting with technology, with his pioneering ultrafine Pleats Please fabrics leading the way. He is also known for breaking the boundaries between Eastern and Western design, winning him a great deal of praise in the fashion world.

31

Moves to New York to work with Geoffrey Beene

32

Returns to Tokyo and founds the Miyake Design Studio, producing luxury womenswear

34

Receives an invitation to show in Paris, and continues showing there for years

33

Shows his first ready-to-wear collection in New York

55

Launches the Pleats Please Issey Miyake collection

59

Launches the A-POC (A Piece of Cloth) clothing line with the help of his long-term design assistant, Dai Fujiwara

THE MIYAKE ISSEY FOUNDATION

66

Establishes The Miyake Issey Foundation to enrich design culture in Japan

61

Hands over design of his ready-to-wear lines to assistant Naoki Takizawa, and returns to researching full-time

Receives Japan's Order of Culture honor from Emperor Akihito

75

Launches Homme Plissé Issey Miyake, which offers contemporary menswear

78

Stages a major retrospective at Tokyo's National Art Center: "The Work of Miyake Issey"

KENZO TAKADA

DATE OF BIRTH
27 February 1939

BIRTHPLACE
Japan

LABEL
Kenzo

> "Fashion is like eating. You shouldn't stick with the same menu."

1939

0 — Born in Himeji, Hyogo, Japan to innkeeper parents

$7/MONTH

Works as a painter's apprentice for just US$7 a month

WOMEN ONLY

19 — Becomes the first male student of the previously women-only Bunka Fashion College, against his parents' wishes

JUNGLE JAP

31 — Opens his first boutique, Jungle Jap, and holds his first show there

VOGUE

Next significant development in Paris's scene!

32 — *Vogue* calls his designs the next significant development in the Paris boutique scene

45 — Designs an inexpensive line for The Limited, pioneering mass-market collaborations and leading some high-end retailers to stop stocking his clothing

Launches the Kenzo Jeans and Kenzo Jungle diffusion lines

LVMH $
KENZO

I will retire!
KENZO

47 — Launches Kenzo bed linen and bath accessories

54 — Sells the Kenzo brand to French luxury-goods company LVMH

60 — Announces his retirement to pursue an art career, leaving his assistants in charge of his fashion house

Interested in fashion...

FASHION

Develops an interest in fashion through reading his sister's magazines.

Studies English literature at the University of Kobe Gaibo, but soon drops out

Japanese-born designer Kenzo Takada arrived in Paris with little money, minimal knowledge of the French language, and with no connections. But that did not stop him from leaving a bold, provocative mark on the fashion world. Along with revolutionizing the traditional Paris design scene with a new flavor of exoticism and ethnicity, Takada pioneered the mass-market designer-collaboration trend that's popular today.

Works for the department store Sanai, designing up to 40 styles a month

25
Inspired by a teacher's stories, he takes a boat to Paris, despite not knowing French or having any connections

I sell fashion drawings.

Visits couture houses trying to sell his fashion illustrations to earn a living, and begins to build a network

PISANTI TEXTILE GROUP

I am a freelancer.

26
Works as a designer for the Pisanti Textile Group and Relations Textiles

Becomes a freelance designer

ZURICH

39
Holds shows in a circus tent, creating a lively and informal presentation in stark contrast to the cold, formal Paris scene

40
Showcases a collection in Zurich, Switzerland, for the first time

夢・夢のあと

44
Launches his first men's collection

42
Directs the film "Dream, After Dream"

Launches a fragrance just for fun, and enjoys success with the launch of Flower by Kenzo in 2000

La Redoute
yumē

KENZO TAKADA

63
Starts a new fashion label, Yume, and a bed-linen range for Europe's biggest mail-order company, La Redoute

66
Turns to interiors, and launches a homeware and furniture brand called Gokan Kobo

81
Dies of complications from COVID-19 in Paris

RALPH LAUREN
RALPH RUEBEN LIFSHITZ

DATE OF BIRTH
14 October 1939

BIRTHPLACE
United States of America

LABEL
Ralph Lauren

1939

0 — Born in the Bronx, New York City, to Jewish immigrant parents

Works as a sales assistant at Brooks Brothers while waiting to be drafted into military

Serves in the US Army for 2 years

31 Introduces his womenswear line and launches the now-iconic Polo logoĐ

29 Launches a full menswear line, offering a high-class, Ivy League aesthetic

32 Releases his signature short-sleeved shirt featuring the Polo logo

Gets close to bankruptcy, but saves the business by recruiting business partner Peter Strom and investing his own savings

-$100,000

33 Designs clothing for the film "The Great Gatsby" and, 5 years later, "Annie Hall"

polo.com | Q
ralphlauren.com | Q

61 Launches polo.com, later renamed ralphlauren.com

66 Displays his collection of vintage and rare cars in an exhibition called "Speed, Style and Beauty"

"Style is very personal. It has nothing to do with fashion. Fashion is over quickly. Style is forever."

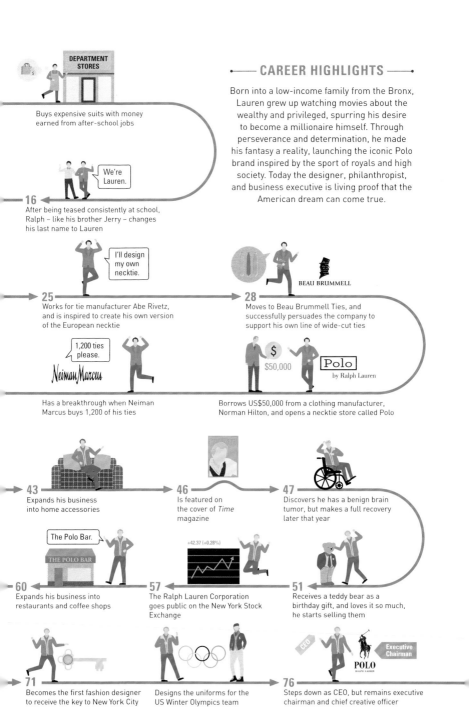

Buys expensive suits with money earned from after-school jobs

We're Lauren.

16
After being teased consistently at school, Ralph – like his brother Jerry – changes his last name to Lauren

Born into a low-income family from the Bronx, Lauren grew up watching movies about the wealthy and privileged, spurring his desire to become a millionaire himself. Through perseverance and determination, he made his fantasy a reality, launching the iconic Polo brand inspired by the sport of royals and high society. Today the designer, philanthropist, and business executive is living proof that the American dream can come true.

I'll design my own necktie.

25
Works for tie manufacturer Abe Rivetz, and is inspired to create his own version of the European necktie

BEAU BRUMMELL

28
Moves to Beau Brummell Ties, and successfully persuades the company to support his own line of wide-cut ties

1,200 ties please.

Neiman Marcus

Has a breakthrough when Neiman Marcus buys 1,200 of his ties

$50,000

Polo
by Ralph Lauren

Borrows US$50,000 from a clothing manufacturer, Norman Hilton, and opens a necktie store called Polo

43
Expands his business into home accessories

46
Is featured on the cover of *Time* magazine

47
Discovers he has a benign brain tumor, but makes a full recovery later that year

The Polo Bar.

THE POLO BAR

60
Expands his business into restaurants and coffee shops

+42.37 (+0.28%)

57
The Ralph Lauren Corporation goes public on the New York Stock Exchange

51
Receives a teddy bear as a birthday gift, and loves it so much, he starts selling them

71
Becomes the first fashion designer to receive the key to New York City

76
Designs the uniforms for the US Winter Olympics team

CEO

POLO
RALPH LAUREN

Executive Chairman

76
Steps down as CEO, but remains executive chairman and chief creative officer

ICONIC ITEMS

BY DESIGNERS BORN DURING THE 1930s

1 POWER SUIT –
GIORGIO ARMANI

Introduced in 1980
Armani presented a deconstructed women's
suit with highly refined menswear fabrics.
The Power Suit came to symbolize an era
of international economic prosperity by
projecting authority and self-confidence.

2 MINISKIRT –
MARY QUANT

Introduced in the 1950s
Quant did not invent the
miniskirt, but she did popularize
it as part of the emerging youth
culture of the 1960s. It was
a rebellious contrast to the
repressed post-war generation,
who were accustomed to no-
frills, functional designs. It also
marked the beginning of the
sexual-liberation movement,
helped along by the invention of
the birth-control pill.

3 HOODED PINK DRESS –
AZZEDINE ALAÏA

Introduced in 1985
Many celebrities – including singer Grace Jones – are
fans of Alaïa's form-fitting clothes, because they give
them sex appeal and confidence. In the 1985 Bond film
"A View to a Kill", Jones wore the designer's hooded pink
dress, which became an icon. Notably, it was replicated
in 2001 by Kylie Minogue in the video for her hit song
"Can't Get You Out of My Head".

4
RED DRESS – VALENTINO GARAVANI

Introduced in 1959
Inspired by a woman wearing red at an opera in Barcelona, Valentino presented gowns in his now signature hue: 100% magenta, 100% yellow, 10% black.

5
PLEATING – ISSEY MIYAKE

Introduced in 1991
Miyake began to experiment with new methods of pleating that would allow both flexibility of movement for the wearer, and ease of care and production. The fabric was first seen in William Forsythe's 1991 ballet "The Loss of Small Detail" for the Frankfurt Ballet, and was developed into the Pleats Please line in 1993.

6
POLO SHIRT – RALPH LAUREN

Introduced in 1972
Brooks Brothers presented the very first button-down polo shirt in 1896, but Lauren's version appealed to a much wider audience. A lifestyle icon of the upper class, the highly profitable Polo shirt turned Ralph Lauren into a powerful brand.

7
LE SMOKING SUIT – YVES SAINT LAURENT

Introduced in 1966
Le Smoking is the first-ever tuxedo for women, and was inspired by men's smoking jackets of the 19th century. While the collection was not well received during its initial launch, it went on to become one of the most important moments in Saint Laurent history.

BORN DURING THE

1940s

The rise in gender equality ushered in a new confidence among women, resulting in the advent of "power dressing" in the workplace. In the art world, a minimalist aesthetic reigned supreme, inspiring fashion designers to follow suit with simple, pared-back designs that signified a reaction against materialism. The rising distaste for overconsumption also reflected the punk and hippie movements, while Japan's flourishing design scene began to redefine fashion with unconventional, anti-modern statements.

ROBERTO CAVALLI

DATE OF BIRTH
15 November 1940

BIRTHPLACE
Italy

LABELS
Roberto Cavalli

1940

0
Born in Florence to a seamstress mother and a mine-surveyor father; his grandfather is a celebrated painter

I am his grandfather, also an Impressionist painter.

24
Marries his first love, Silvanella Giannoni, to humiliate her father, who said Cavalli was not rich enough to be "husband material"

30
Debuts his first ready-to-wear collection in Paris using a patented leather with a revolutionary printing technique

I had this idea to print on leather.

55
Works with Lycra to invent stretch denim

48
Debuts his signature printed jeans, making a comeback

58
Launches Cavalli Jeans (later renamed Just Cavalli), which is aimed at a younger customer, cementing his status as a pioneer in the denim world

62
Opens his first café, Cavalli Caffè, in Florence, revamping it with his signature animal prints

67
Launches a high-street collection for H&M that sells out in hours

65
Launches Roberto Cavalli Vodka, with a snakeskin-print bottle

Revamps Playboy's famous bunny costumes

68
Opens his first nightclub, in Dubai

70
Holds an extravagant celebrity- and model-filled Parisian party to celebrate 40 years of business, and releases a coffee-table book

"Excess is success."

ACADEMY OF ART IN FLORENCE

17
Studies at the Academy of Art in Florence, following in the footsteps of his grandfather

— CAREER HIGHLIGHTS —

Too much is never enough in the world of Roberto Cavalli, the grandson of Italian painter Giuseppe Rossi. He first found success by inventing a new method for painting on fabric, and soon developed skills for fashion printing. Although he has had his fair share of critics, they never stopped him from pushing forward. Cavalli built a maximalist fashion empire, earning the nickname "the King of Excess".

20
Begins a career as a textile printer for an Italian knitwear line

Earns a commission from Hermès and Pierre Cardin to use his patented technique

34
Divorces Giannoni

Don't destroy the femininity of a woman.

roberto cavalli
Creative Director

Experiences an unprofitable decade due to the rise of minimalistic and deconstructed fashion

40
Marries Düringer, who becomes Roberto Cavalli creative director

37
Sits on the judging panel for the Miss Universe pageant, and starts a relationship with second-place winner Eva Düringer

Releases his first fragrance, Roberto Cavalli Parfum, which features a snakeskin-print bottle; the fragrance was originally called Serpentine

TAX FRAUD

Appears in court after Italian authorities charge him with tax fraud; he clears the case 6 years later

Sponsors the exhibition "Wild: Fashion Untamed" at the Metropolitan Museum of Art's Costume Institute in New York

I am sorry...

It's too bad!

64
Withdraws and apologizes for a line of women's underwear featuring Hindu goddesses, which is sharply criticized by Hindus all over the world

⊙ TARGET

72
Launches a second high-street line, this time for Target Australia

I need rest...

Creative Director

73
Steps down from the role of creative director, for health reasons

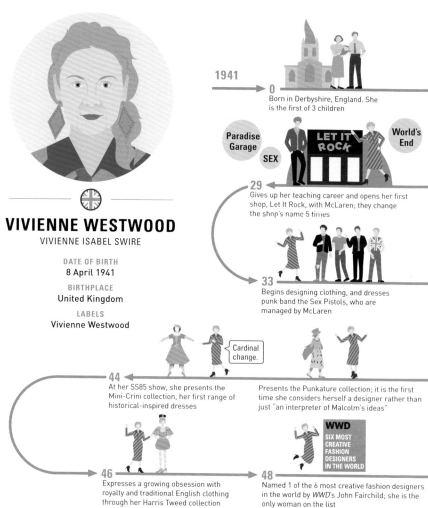

VIVIENNE WESTWOOD

VIVIENNE ISABEL SWIRE

DATE OF BIRTH
8 April 1941

BIRTHPLACE
United Kingdom

LABELS
Vivienne Westwood

1941

0
Born in Derbyshire, England. She is the first of 3 children

Paradise Garage

SEX

LET IT ROCK

World's End

29
Gives up her teaching career and opens her first shop, Let It Rock, with McLaren; they change the shop's name 5 times

33
Begins designing clothing, and dresses punk band the Sex Pistols, who are managed by McLaren

Cardinal change.

44
At her SS85 show, she presents the Mini-Crini collection, her first range of historical-inspired dresses

Presents the Punkature collection; it is the first time she considers herself a designer rather than just "an interpreter of Malcolm's ideas"

46
Expresses a growing obsession with royalty and traditional English clothing through her Harris Tweed collection

48
Named 1 of the 6 most creative fashion designers in the world by *WWD*'s John Fairchild; she is the only woman on the list

WWD
SIX MOST CREATIVE FASHION DESIGNERS IN THE WORLD

"My clothes have a story. They have an identity. They have a character and a purpose. That's why they become classics. Because they keep on telling a story. They are still telling it."

ACTIVE RESISTANCE TO PROPAGANDA

66
Releases a manifesto, "Active Resistance to Propaganda", raising awareness of environmental and human-rights issues

$ £350,000 TAX

HM Revenue & Customs

70
Agrees to pay almost £350,000 in tax to Her Majesty's Revenue and Customs for significantly underestimating the value of her brand

17 Moves to London and studies silversmithing at Harrow School of Art at Westminster University, but leaves after just 1 term

18 Eventually becomes a primary-school teacher, and sells jewelry on the side at Portobello Road Market

22 Meets Malcolm McLaren; he becomes her romantic and business partner, and transforms her life

21 Marries Derek Westwood; they divorce 3 years later

40 Shows her first commercial ready-to-wear collection, Pirate, distinguishing herself from the mainstream, power-dressing style

Professional partners.

42 Ends her romantic relationship with McLaren, but they remain business partners for another 5 years. Takes the bold step of starting to show in Paris

— CAREER HIGHLIGHTS —

Westwood's rebellious attitude is legendary. With the help of Malcolm McLaren – the self-proclaimed inventor of punk – Westwood started her career dressing the Sex Pistols. She is considered largely responsible for bringing modern punk and new wave fashion into the mainstream, with her provocative designs communicating her political and environmental stances. The attention her radical designs have received has helped her build a vast and successful business empire.

49 Launches a menswear collection

52 At the AW93 show, Naomi Campbell falls over while wearing the 9-inch Ghillie heels

Marries longtime design partner Andreas Kronthaler, who is 25 years her junior

65 Advances to Dame, 14 years later after receiving the title of Officer of the Order of the British Empire; she confides that she is not wearing knickers

63 The V&A mounts a retrospective, "Vivienne Westwood: 34 Years in Fashion"; it is the largest-ever exhibition for a living British designer

62 Sends men down the catwalk wearing fake breasts

71 Launches Climate Revolution, declaring that stopping climate change is now her priority

77 Collaborates with Burberry on a limited-edition collection of reimagined British heritage pieces

REI KAWAKUBO

DATE OF BIRTH
11 October 1942

BIRTHPLACE
Japan

LABELS
Comme des Garçons

— CAREER HIGHLIGHTS —

The famously reclusive Kawakubo started her brand without any formal training and ran it independently, without financial support. Challenging the definitions of glamour and beauty, Kawakubo pushed the boundaries of fashion with a daring aesthetic – one that made her stand out during the 1980s, when office clothing was at the height of popularity. A woman of few words, Kawakubo prefers to let her designs speak for themselves.

1942

Trained English teacher.

Administrator at Keio University.

0
Born in Tokyo; her father is an administrator at Keio University, and her mother teaches English

MINAMI-AOYAMA DISTRICT

33
Opens her first boutique, in Tokyo's Minami-Aoyama district

36
Adds a menswear line, Homme Comme des Garçons, which is soon followed by lines including Tricot, Robe de Chambre, and Noir

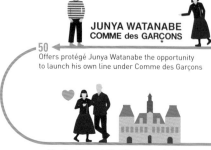

JUNYA WATANABE
COMME des GARÇONS

50
Offers protégé Junya Watanabe the opportunity to launch his own line under Comme des Garçons

Marries Adrian Joffe, 10 years her junior, at Paris City Hall

62
Kick-starts a global trend by opening pop-up shops around the globe

COMME des GARÇONS

60
Adds a streetwear line, Comme des Garçons PLAY

DOVER STREET MARKET

Launches her first multi-brand shop, Dover Street Market, in London – and later in other cities

66
Collaborates with H&M on a collection that's so in demand, fans camp outside stores to buy it

67
Presents an affordable collection, BLACK, referencing past bestsellers

B-ack
COMME des GARÇONS

Being rebellious, Kawakubo bunches her school-uniform socks down to her ankles

22
Studies fine arts and aesthetics, and graduates from Keio University in Tokyo

Like a boy!

COMME des GARÇONS

Involved in styling photo shoots for ad campaigns.

27
Sells designs under the label Comme des Garçons

Works in the advertising department of a textile factory, leaving 3 years later to become a freelance stylist

Begins a romantic relationship with Yohji Yamamoto, but it does not last long

39
Presents her first fashion collection, Destroy in Paris, shocking critics

Six

46
Launches the magazine *Six*, a biannual large-format publication, which runs for 13 years

Takes the concept of the atelier lab coat and creates long black jackets for her runway show staff, which they wear for a number of seasons

41
Involved in the exhibition "A New Wave in Fashion: Three Japanese Designers" along with Yohji Yamamoto and Issey Miyake at the Phoenix Art Museum

54
Becomes guest editor of high-art publication *Visionaire*

"For something to be beautiful it doesn't have to be pretty."

54
Presents her best-known collection, Body Meets Dress – Dress Meets Body, featuring padded clothing

Second living designer after YSL.

70
Explores 2D surfaces in her AW12 collection

75
Stages "Rei Kawakubo/Comme des Garçons: Art of the In-Between" at the Metropolitan Museum of Art Costume Institute in New York

CALVIN KLEIN
CALVIN RICHARD KLEIN

DATE OF BIRTH
19 November 1942

BIRTHPLACE
United States of America

LABEL
Calvin Klein

1942

0
Born into a Jewish family in New York; he was the second of 3 children

26
A buyer accidentally walks into Klein's workroom, resulting in the brand's first big order

32
Divorces Centre and starts partying hard

Do you know what comes between me and my Calvins? Nothing.

38
Airs a controversial TV ad featuring a 15-year-old Brooke Shields, which wildly increases the brand's profits

36
Gives up his partying lifestyle after his daughter, Marci Klein, is kidnapped and held for US$100,000 ransom

$500,000

40
Introduces men's underwear with a US$500,000 ad campaign by Bruce Weber; places an enormous billboard in New York's Times Square

SALES

It's an underwear revolution.

Launches menswear-inspired underwear for women and sells 80,000 pairs in 90 days

41
Acquires Puritan Fashion Corporation for jeans licensing; however, sales plummet dramatically

Calvin Klein

50
Reorganizes the company with the help of music mogul David Geffen

Rehab Center

46
Struggles with drug and alcohol abuse, and checks himself into rehab

Bad influence!

Launches a provocative ad campaign featuring Mark Wahlberg and Kate Moss

53
Presents a series of controversial ads featuring adolescents, but removes them after negative feedback and an investigation by the US Justice Department

Sketches and sews while other boys play sports

18 Studies at the Fashion Institute of Technology in New York

I don't like this job.

20 Works for a series of middle- to down-market manufacturers, and loathes the products

Calvin Klein

26 Founds Calvin Klein Ltd with his childhood friend Barry Schwartz, initially designing only coats

You're fired!

Starts creating his own collection on his kitchen table, and is fired when his boss finds out

22 Marries textile designer Jayne Centre

SALES

Designs his tight-fitting signature jeans, which gross US$200,000 in their first week of sales

The largest amount we'd ever spent.

43 Spends US$13 million to advertise his second fragrance, Obsession, which becomes a bestseller

44 Marries his assistant, Kelly Rector, but they live separately until their divorce in 2006, seeming to confirm the rumor that he is bisexual

"Anything I wanted to do, I did. If there's something I want to do, nothing stops me."

—— CAREER HIGHLIGHTS ——

Calvin Klein's distinctively clean, casual-chic aesthetic helped lift America's fashion credibility on a global scale. Klein pushed boundaries with provocative commercials, creating a fashion-advertising revolution. While his career and his personal life did not always run smoothly, he faced negativity and criticism head-on, never giving up.

Launches CK One, one of the first fragrances marketed as unisex

Calvin Klein → PVH

60 Sells Calvin Klein Ltd. to Phillips-Van Heusen Corporation, and retires

68 Starts a relationship with ex-porn star Nick Gruber, but they separate after 2 years

YOHJI YAMAMOTO

DATE OF BIRTH
3 October 1943

BIRTHPLACE
Japan

LABEL
Yohji Yamamoto

CAREER HIGHLIGHTS

Yamamoto is known for his avant-garde designs and distinctly Japanese aesthetic. In stark contrast to the trend-driven fashions of the 80s, Yamamoto's unique point of view disrupted the fashion scene in a positive way. Unfortunately, masterful designs aren't always enough, and the designer came close to bankruptcy due to poor financial management in the 2000s. Today, the designer says he cannot imagine retiring.

"I think perfection is ugly. Somewhere in the things humans make, I want to see scars, failure, disorder, distortion."

1943

0
Born in Tokyo during WWII

World War II

I want to help you, mama!

Helps his mother by working at her dressmaking shop while learning tailoring skills

I want women in men's style.

26
Graduates from Bunka Fashion College, and wins a fashion prize to go to Paris

41
Presents his first Yohji Yamamoto Pour Homme collection, creating new classicism for menswear

47
Begins designing costumes for operas, first for Puccini's "Madame Butterfly"

61
Receives the Medal with Purple Ribbon from the Japanese government

$100 MILLION   Y's

65
Sales of Yamamoto's 2 main lines –
Yohji Yamamoto and Y's – average more than US$100 million annually

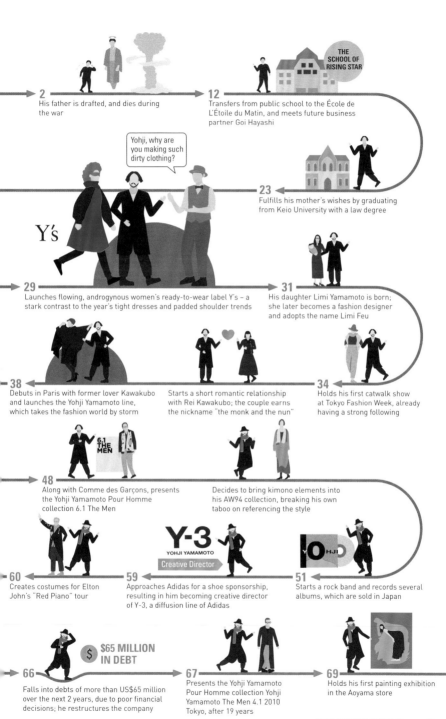

2
His father is drafted, and dies during the war

12
Transfers from public school to the École de L'Étoile du Matin, and meets future business partner Goi Hayashi

THE SCHOOL OF RISING STAR

Yohji, why are you making such dirty clothing?

23
Fulfills his mother's wishes by graduating from Keio University with a law degree

Y's

29
Launches flowing, androgynous women's ready-to-wear label Y's – a stark contrast to the year's tight dresses and padded shoulder trends

31
His daughter Limi Yamamoto is born; she later becomes a fashion designer and adopts the name Limi Feu

38
Debuts in Paris with former lover Kawakubo and launches the Yohji Yamamoto line, which takes the fashion world by storm

Starts a short romantic relationship with Rei Kawakubo; the couple earns the nickname "the monk and the nun"

34
Holds his first catwalk show at Tokyo Fashion Week, already having a strong following

48
Along with Comme des Garçons, presents the Yohji Yamamoto Pour Homme collection 6.1 The Men

Decides to bring kimono elements into his AW94 collection, breaking his own taboo on referencing the style

60
Creates costumes for Elton John's "Red Piano" tour

59
Approaches Adidas for a shoe sponsorship, resulting in him becoming creative director of Y-3, a diffusion line of Adidas

Y-3
YOHJI YAMAMOTO
Creative Director

51
Starts a rock band and records several albums, which are sold in Japan

66
Falls into debts of more than US$65 million over the next 2 years, due to poor financial decisions; he restructures the company

$65 MILLION IN DEBT

67
Presents the Yohji Yamamoto Pour Homme collection Yohji Yamamoto The Men 4.1 2010 Tokyo, after 19 years

69
Holds his first painting exhibition in the Aoyama store

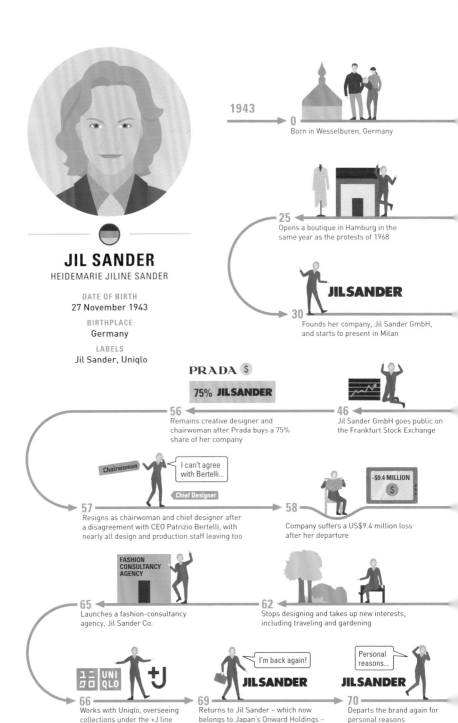

JIL SANDER
HEIDEMARIE JILINE SANDER

DATE OF BIRTH
27 November 1943

BIRTHPLACE
Germany

LABELS
Jil Sander, Uniqlo

1943

0
Born in Wesselburen, Germany

25
Opens a boutique in Hamburg in the same year as the protests of 1968

JILSANDER

30
Founds her company, Jil Sander GmbH, and starts to present in Milan

PRADA $

75% **JILSANDER**

56
Remains creative designer and chairwoman after Prada buys a 75% share of her company

46
Jil Sander GmbH goes public on the Frankfurt Stock Exchange

Chairwoman

I can't agree with Bertelli...

Chief Designer

57
Resigns as chairwoman and chief designer after a disagreement with CEO Patrizio Bertelli, with nearly all design and production staff leaving too

58
Company suffers a US$9.4 million loss after her departure

-$9.4 MILLION

FASHION CONSULTANCY AGENCY

65
Launches a fashion-consultancy agency, Jil Sander Co.

62
Stops designing and takes up new interests, including traveling and gardening

UNI QLO +J

66
Works with Uniqlo, overseeing collections under the +J line for 2 years

I'm back again!

JILSANDER

69
Returns to Jil Sander – which now belongs to Japan's Onward Holdings – after Raf Simons leaves

Personal reasons...

JILSANDER

70
Departs the brand again for personal reasons

Maintains a good relationship with her father and half-brother after her parents' divorce

18 Studies at the Krefeld School of Textiles in Germany

20 Enrolls at the University of California as a foreign exchange student while working as a fashion journalist for *McCall's* magazine

Becomes fashion editor at *Petra* magazine in Germany

HAMBURG

21 Returns to Hamburg after her father dies unexpectedly

QUEEN OF LESS

Vanity Fair dubs Sander "the Queen of Less"

31 Debuts her first collection, which sells out in just 1 week

32 Receives negative feedback on her debut collection in Paris, and does not show for the next 11 years

35 Named one of the 12 best designers in the world by Japanese magazine *High Fashion*

I'm back!

CHIEF DESIGNER **JIL SANDER**

60 Returns to Jil Sander just in time for the SS04 collection, and signs a 6-year contract with Prada

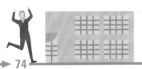

Bye again!

PRADA **JIL SANDER**

61 Resigns from her post again after 18 months and terminates the contract with Prada due to insurmountable differences with Bertelli

74 Her first solo exhibition opens at the Museum Angewandte Kunst in Frankfurt

"I am convinced that there can be luxury in simplicity."

——— CAREER HIGHLIGHTS ———

Whether in her work or her personal life, Sander has never been ostentatious. A pioneer of the clean, minimalist clothing trend, Sander earned the nickname "the Queen of Less". By focusing on luxurious textiles and quality craftsmanship, she has defined a clear point of view and, in turn, made her designs a staple of smart, intelligent women's wardrobes.

PAUL SMITH
PAUL BRIERLEY SMITH

DATE OF BIRTH
5 July 1946

BIRTHPLACE
United Kingdom

LABEL
Paul Smith

1946 → 0
Born in Nottingham, England

Attends evening tailoring classes, later joining
Lincroft Kilgour in Savile Row

Paul Smith Vêtements
pour Hommes

24
Opens his first tiny shop in Nottingham
with the encouragement of wife-to-be
Pauline Denyer

Young creative
favourite.

Creates a signature suit style that
becomes a favorite among young
creatives in London

Paul Smith
retail style.

Becomes a pioneer of men's lifestyle stores
thanks to a talent for creating innovative
retail concepts

JAPAN

38
Signs a licensing deal in Japan, which
later becomes his biggest market

47
Introduces a women's collection after discovering
that women purchase 15% of his clothes

63
Dresses the Manchester United
football team

Dresses athletes, including professional cyclist Sir
Chris Hoy and Olympic medal winner Bradley Wiggins

64
Opens his first standalone
womenswear store in Mayfair, London

66
Collaborates with the Isle of Man Post Office,
designing a collection of 7 stamps for the London
2012 Olympic and Paralympic Games

Dreams of becoming
a professional cyclist

Pursues his new passion,
becoming a menswear buyer

During his 6-month hospital stay, he makes
new friends, who introduce him to the world of
art and fashion

16
Drops out of school and begins working
in a clothing warehouse as an errand
boy, cycling to work every day

17
Injures himself in a bike crash,
ending his racing ambitions

30
Shows his first menswear
collection in Paris

33
Opens the first Paul Smith store in
Covent Garden, London; it is the first
fashion shop in the area

"Don't dress for fashion, dress for yourself."

— CAREER HIGHLIGHTS —

Hoping to become a professional racing cyclist from a
young age, Smith changed his focus after he was involved
in a serious bike accident. In a serendipitous series of
events, his time in hospital led him to fashion. Starting off
with his own boutique, he learned the business side of the
industry, before honing his craft with impeccably tailored
British pieces. The designer eventually built an empire
with iconic designs inspired by traditional menswear, and
a splash of quirky colored stripes.

54
Awarded a knighthood by
the Queen, and marries Denyer

62
Contributes to Vogue.com as
a guest blogger

60
Incorporates his now signature stripes
into his collections

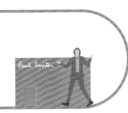

Paints his new store in LA shocking pink;
it later becomes an Instagram hot spot

67
Celebrates 40 years in fashion with the
exhibition "Hello, My Name Is Paul Smith"

Decides to refine his logo, using his
signature stripes to avoid fixed branding

GIANNI VERSACE
GIOVANNI MARIA VERSACE

DATE OF BIRTH
2 December 1946

BIRTHPLACE
Italy

LABEL
Versace

"I hate designers who live in an ivory tower. I think you have to be part of this culture, of this music, of our time. If you understand your time, you are a good designer."

1946

0
Born in Reggio Calabria, Italy, to a dressmaker mother

22
Continues to work in his mother's studio as both a designer and a buyer, creating decorative embroidery

26
Moves to Milan and works as a freelance fashion designer for an upscale brand

Meets model Antonio D'Amico, who remains Versace's life partner until his death

45
The world's top models walk Versace's catwalk together, giving rise to the term "supermodel"

Versace is diagnosed with a rare cancer of the inner ear, but recovers

47
Launches a furniture and homeware line, Versace Home

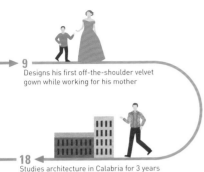

9
Designs his first off-the-shoulder velvet gown while working for his mother

18
Studies architecture in Calabria for 3 years

Versace was a game-changer. His designs fused glamorous supermodel style and popular American culture with pioneering fabrics and innovative technology. The refreshing contrast to simplistic mainstream fashion built him a globally recognized fashion empire in less than 10 years. After his life was tragically cut short, the designer's family – most famously his sister Donatella – has continued to run his empire.

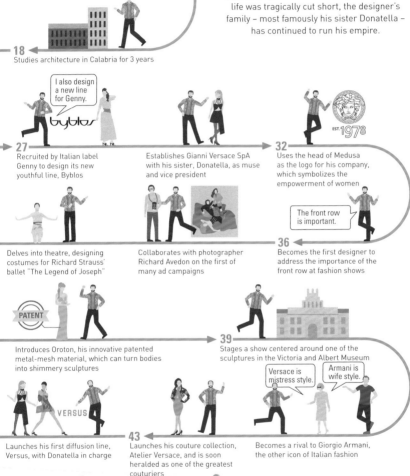

I also design a new line for Genny.

byblos

27
Recruited by Italian label Genny to design its new youthful line, Byblos

Establishes Gianni Versace SpA with his sister, Donatella, as muse and vice president

EST. 1978

32
Uses the head of Medusa as the logo for his company, which symbolizes the empowerment of women

The front row is important.

Delves into theatre, designing costumes for Richard Strauss' ballet "The Legend of Joseph"

Collaborates with photographer Richard Avedon on the first of many ad campaigns

36
Becomes the first designer to address the importance of the front row at fashion shows

PATENT

Introduces Oroton, his innovative patented metal-mesh material, which can turn bodies into shimmery sculptures

39
Stages a show centered around one of the sculptures in the Victoria and Albert Museum

Versace is mistress style.

Armani is wife style.

VERSUS

Launches his first diffusion line, Versus, with Donatella in charge

43
Launches his couture collection, Atelier Versace, and is soon heralded as one of the greatest couturiers

Becomes a rival to Giorgio Armani, the other icon of Italian fashion

48
Elizabeth Hurley wears Versace's "safety-pin dress", which becomes one of the most famous red-carpet gowns of all time

49
Creates an iconic moment when Kate Moss wears a sparkling silver wedding dress for the finale of his AW95 show

GIANNI VERSACE

50
Shot dead in front of his Miami Beach mansion by serial killer Andrew Cunanan

DIANE VON FURSTENBERG

DIANE SIMONE MICHELLE HALFIN

DATE OF BIRTH
31 December 1946

BIRTHPLACE
Belgium

LABEL
Diane von Furstenberg

─── CAREER HIGHLIGHTS ───

Thanks to the overnight success of her wrap dress when she was just 27, von Furstenberg became a poster child for the American dream. The designer still faced difficulties: her business's financial struggles and a terrifying diagnosis of cancer. As a strong, independent woman who knew "fear is not an option", she fought back, relying on her instincts, passion and determination to reach the position she is in today.

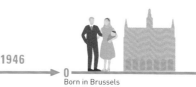

1946

0
Born in Brussels

Sees one of her wrap tops and one of her skirts on TV and decides to combine the 2 garments into 1

27
Debuts what is to become her phenomenally popular wrap dress

43
Moves back to the United States and settles on a farm in Connecticut

51
Diagnosed with tongue cancer

59
Named President of the Council of Fashion Designers of America

55
Marries her longtime friend, American media mogul Barry Diller

64
Launches the DVF Awards to honor women who display leadership and courage

65
Launches a diffusion line, reissuing vintage prints in classic styles

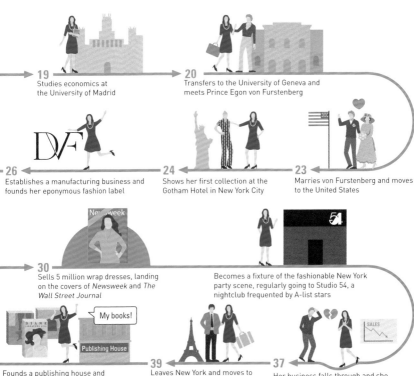

19
Studies economics at the University of Madrid

20
Transfers to the University of Geneva and meets Prince Egon von Furstenberg

26
Establishes a manufacturing business and founds her eponymous fashion label

24
Shows her first collection at the Gotham Hotel in New York City

23
Marries von Furstenberg and moves to the United States

30
Sells 5 million wrap dresses, landing on the covers of *Newsweek* and *The Wall Street Journal*

Becomes a fixture of the fashionable New York party scene, regularly going to Studio 54, a nightclub frequented by A-list stars

Founds a publishing house and publishes a series of books including "Beds", "The Bath", "The Table" and "Diane: A Signature Life"

39
Leaves New York and moves to Paris to live with Italian novelist Alain Elkann

37
Her business falls through and she divorces Egon von Furstenberg

"I did not know what I wanted to do, but I knew the kind of woman I wanted to become."

Relaunches the brand, and makes a triumphant comeback with a wrap dress that features subtle new details

67
Showcases her collection with Google Glasses on the runway

68
Releases her memoir, "The Woman I Wanted to Be"

Premieres her own reality show, "House of DVF"

DONNA KARAN
DONNA IVY FASKE

DATE OF BIRTH
2 October 1948

BIRTHPLACE
United States of America

LABELS
Anne Klein, Donna Karan New York

1948

I'm a model.

I'm a tailor.

0
Born in Forest Hills, New York,
to a tailor father and a model mother

20
Attends Parsons School of Design and gets
a summer job at Anne Klein & Co

Becomes an assistant designer at Anne Klein,
and eventually becomes chief assistant

34
Marries Weiss, who later becomes
Co-CEO

30
Divorces Mark Karan

Bye!

36
Leaves Anne Klein and starts her own business
with Weiss and backing from a Japanese company

37
Shows her first women's
clothing collection

Chairwoman

CEO

+53.53 (+0.34%)

52
Leaves CEO position, but continues as chairwoman
and designer for the Donna Karan main line

48
Donna Karan International goes public on
the New York Stock Exchange

I lost my
other half...

The brand is acquired by LVMH

53
Retreats after Weiss dies
of lung cancer

59
Founds Urban Zen, an independent,
socially conscious ready-to-wear brand

14
Begins selling clothes

"Delete the negative; accentuate the positive!"

18
Graduates from Hewlett High School

With a tailor father and model mother, fashion was ingrained in Karan's life. During her younger years, she was taught by her parents to pay attention to detail and look for inspiration in unlikely places. Thanks to her hugely successful capsule collection of 7 easy-to-wear wardrobe staples, paired with brilliant marketing, Karan was crowned "the Queen of Seventh Avenue".

22
While married to Mark Karan, starts a relationship with artist Stephan Weiss

Seven easy pieces.

We are head designers.

25
After Klein's death, Karan is promoted to head designer of Anne Klein & Co during her pregnancy, along with former schoolmate Louis Dell'Olio

Becomes well-known for creating a capsule collection built around 7 interchangeable pieces that suit all occasions

DKNY
DONNA KARAN NEW YORK

41
Launches a popular diffusion brand for younger customers, DKNY, designing with her daughter Gabby in mind

40
Nicknamed "the Queen of Seventh Avenue"

aka @DKNYPRGIRL

Focus on urban Zen

61
Becomes the first designer to tap into a single personality to run the brand's social media, inventing @DKNYprgirl

67
Announces she is stepping down as head of her company to focus on Urban Zen

MIUCCIA PRADA
MARIA BIANCHI PRADA

DATE OF BIRTH
10 May 1949

BIRTHPLACE
Italy

LABEL
Prada

1949

0
Born in Milan

Call me Miuccia.

FRATELLI PRADA
VALIGERIE

26
Born Maria Bianchi, she takes the name Miuccia and joins the family's luxury leather goods company, Fratelli Prada

28
Meets her future husband, Patrizio Bertelli, who owns a Tuscan leather-goods factory

Launches her first menswear line

46
Establishes Fondazione Prada, a non-profit institution dedicated to contemporary art and culture

These belong to Prada.

JILSANDER
HELMUT LANG

LVMH
$ FENDI

50
Presents the pivotal SS96 collection, which kick-starts Prada's association with the unexpected and season-defining print

Takes over the fashion houses of Jil Sander and Helmut Lang until their resale in 2006

Joins LVMH to buy Fendi's shares, selling them in 2001

"What you wear is how
you present yourself
to the world, especially today,
when human contacts
are so quick. Fashion
is an instant language."

63
Showcases works in an exhibition called "Schiaparelli and Prada: Impossible Conversations"

PRADASPHERE

65
Stages an exhibition, "Pradasphere" showcasing Prada's obsessions and archives

UNIVERSITÀ DEGLI STUDI DI MILANO

24
Earns a PhD in political science from the University of Milan

Miuccia Prada is one of the highest-paid people in the fashion industry, and one of the most influential women in the world. What started as a small family business grew into a successful empire thanks to her unique combination of intellect and eccentricity. Her nylon handbags with triangular metal badges are iconic and still much-loved.

Starts training as a mime while working at the Teatro Piccolo for 5 years; her rebellious personality begins to show

It's my nickname.

36
Introduces a black nylon backpack, which becomes an enduring icon

39
Debuts her women's ready-to-wear collection

43
Introduces Miu Miu, a secondary line named after her moniker and based on her personal wardrobe

$30 MILLION

Takes inspiration from the iconic nylon backpack and creates a whole collection around it

Grows her business rapidly, transforming it into a fashion empire worth US$30 million

Acquires historic British footwear brand Church's

55
Releases first Prada fragrance

58
Launches Prada touchscreen phone with electronics brand LG

HK

HIGHEST-PAID PEOPLE IN FASHION

Prada goes public in Hong Kong

62
Becomes the highest-paid person in fashion, after declaring her earnings of US$11.3 million

Co-CEO

79TH MOST POWERFUL WOMAN

Together with her husband, becomes Co-CEO of the Prada company

Declared the 79th most powerful woman in the world by *Forbes*

ICONIC ITEMS

BY DESIGNERS BORN DURING THE 1940s

1
PROVOCATIVE ADS –
CALVIN KLEIN

Introduced in 1982
Calvin Klein's advertisements might just
be more famous than his designs. Hiring
Bruce Weber for US$500,000 to create
a provocative ad campaign to announce
his new product line, Klein turned his
underwear into a status symbol, and its
wearers into sex symbols.

2
SAFETY-PIN DRESS –
GIANNI VERSACE

Introduced in 1994
One of Versace's best-known creations, the
"safety-pin" dress, received coverage in
newspapers and magazines around the world
when Elizabeth Hurley wore it to the 1994
premiere of "Four Weddings and a Funeral".
Today, the dress is credited with changing red-
carpet fashion and launching Hurley's career.

3
WRAP DRESS –
DIANE VON FURSTENBERG

Introduced in 1994
Diane von Furstenberg created a versatile
design that had just as much appeal as
comfortable business attire as it did elegant
evening attire. Due to its wide-reaching
popularity, the wrap dress came to be seen
as a symbol of women's liberation in the
1970s, and 5 million of the dresses were
sold within 2 years.

4 LUMP DRESS – REI KAWAKUBO

Introduced in 1996

Kawakubo's statement-making Body Meets Dress – Dress Meets Body collection (widely remembered as the Lumps and Bumps collection) tackled the cultural tropes of female body image. Although not well received by much of the fashion press, it became a collectible piece of design history.

5 NYLON BACKPACK – MIUCCIA PRADA

Introduced in 1984

Miuccia Prada started working with nylon shortly after she took over her grandfather's business in the late 1970s. However, it was the launch of her nylon backpack in 1985 that propelled her career. Made from parachute fabric, the practical, easy-to-wear bag developed a cult following and is still popular today.

6 GHILLIE HEELS – VIVIENNE WESTWOOD

Introduced in 1993

The Ghillie heels are the most famous of all Westwood's footwear designs. A recreation of historical ribbon-lace styles from the 18th and 19th centuries, the 9-inch heels made international news in 1993 when Naomi Campbell suffered a spectacular fall on the catwalk while modeling them.

BORN DURING THE

1950s

With the rise of the internet, fashion designers born in the 1950s began to take a more globalized approach to their designs. Streetwear trends including grunge and hip-hop became a dominant influence on designers, and recycling the trends of previous decades was also common. Designers started to push back against mainstream trends and the fashion system in general, giving rise to an avant-garde and experimental style.

FRANCO MOSCHINO

DATE OF BIRTH
27 February 1950

BIRTHPLACE
Italy

LABEL
Moschino

— CAREER HIGHLIGHTS —

Known for his humorous designs and outspoken comments, Moschino stressed that he was a decorator, not a fashion designer. The "bad boy" of Italian fashion saw clothing as his canvas, constantly shocking his audiences with outrageous ideas that were a protest against the industry. Drawing on pop-culture influences, Moschino defined a decade by mocking high-fashion brands – and even his customers – through his creations.

1950

0
Born in Lombardy, Italy

I need to earn money for my studies.

Works as a freelance fashion illustrator to finance his studies

21
Works as a sketch artist at Versace for 6 years

Becomes the first major designer to use faux fur in his Fun Fur collection

Undergoes surgery for an abdominal tumor

42
Launches his first social-awareness ad campaign

No more fashion shows, private showings only.

Decides to stop having runway presentations, and replaces them with private showings

43
Presents his final show, a 10-year retrospective with a finale of men, women and children dressed in white and wearing AIDS ribbons

Stages a retrospective exhibition, "X Years of Kaos!" at Milan's Museo della Permanente

Draws crazy pictures in the deposits of dust on walls

"Good taste doesn't exist. It is our taste. We have to be proud of it."

18

Runs away from home and moves to Milan to study fine art at Brera Academy

MILAN

27

Designs for Italian label Cadette

33

Starts his own company, Moonshadow, and launches the Moschino Couture label

Creates a sensation by dressing model Pat Cleveland in a silk evening dress, trainers, and a shopping bag

38

Introduces the diffusion line Cheap and Chic

36

Launches the first Moschino Jeans womenswear collection

35

Debuts his first men's collection in Milan

Publishes the book "Moschino. To be, or not to be, that's fashion!"

39

Exhibits artwork at his Milan flagship store, which is converted into a temporary art gallery for the event.

"Waist of money!"

Presents a suit jacket embroidered with the words "waist of money", mocking Chanel's design

41

Presents an ironic Survival Jacket for SS91: it is a khaki military jacket equipped with beauty accessories

44

Presents his final eco-friendly collection under the Nature Friendly Garment label

I'll raise money for the Accademia.

Produces hand-painted garments that are auctioned to raise money for the Accademia Italiana delle Arti at a self-sponsored exhibition

44

Dies of AIDS at the country house in Annone, Italy, where he lived and worked

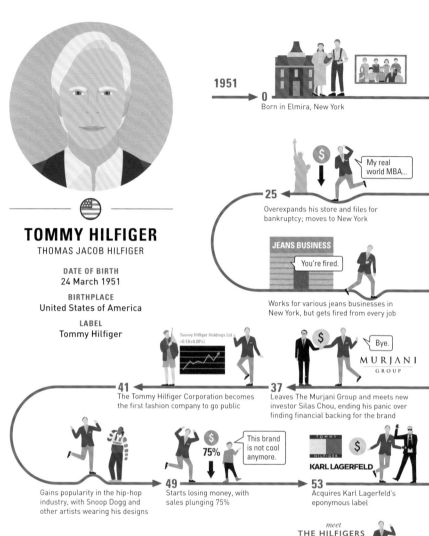

TOMMY HILFIGER
THOMAS JACOB HILFIGER

DATE OF BIRTH
24 March 1951

BIRTHPLACE
United States of America

LABEL
Tommy Hilfiger

1951
0
Born in Elmira, New York

My real world MBA...

25
Overexpands his store and files for bankruptcy; moves to New York

JEANS BUSINESS
You're fired.

Works for various jeans businesses in New York, but gets fired from every job

Bye.

MURJANI GROUP

Tommy Hilfiger Holdings Ltd
+0.13(+0.20%)

41
The Tommy Hilfiger Corporation becomes the first fashion company to go public

37
Leaves The Murjani Group and meets new investor Silas Chou, ending his panic over finding financial backing for the brand

Gains popularity in the hip-hop industry, with Snoop Dogg and other artists wearing his designs

This brand is not cool anymore.

75%

49
Starts losing money, with sales plunging 75%

KARL LAGERFELD

53
Acquires Karl Lagerfeld's eponymous label

meet
THE HILFIGERS

NOAH   CHLOE

Launches the "Meet the Hilfigers" ad campaign online and in-store, showcasing models of different ages and ethnicities

This could be my first hotel.

60
Buys the MetLife Clock Tower with a business partner, and plans to transform it into his brand's first hotel

"Always stay focused. Always give and try your best."

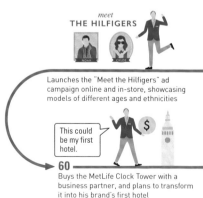

Wears vintage outfits heavily influenced by rock stars, prompting friends to buy pieces from him

— CAREER HIGHLIGHTS —

Hilfiger started his career young, with just a few hundred dollars to his name. After his first store went bankrupt, he learned that the business side of the industry is just as important as the creative side, and adapted accordingly.

Hilfiger went on to build one of the world's most widely recognized and distributed brands, with the colors red, white and blue becoming synonymous with the label. In recent years, he has adapted yet again by teaming up with one of the world's most influential models, Gigi Hadid.

20
Decides to use his life savings – US$150 –
to open a hippie clothing store with 2 friends
in downtown Elmira

28
Sets up a design company called Tommy Hill,
and spends time in India to learn the trade

29
Marries Susie Alexandria
Richard, an employee in his first
store; they divorce in 2000

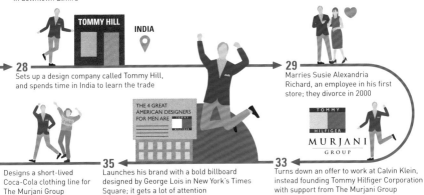

35
Launches his brand with a bold billboard
designed by George Lois in New York's Times
Square; it gets a lot of attention

Designs a short-lived
Coca-Cola clothing line for
The Murjani Group

33
Turns down an offer to work at Calvin Klein,
instead founding Tommy Hilfiger Corporation
with support from The Murjani Group

European market!

Apax PARTNERS
$ **$1.6 BILLION**

54
Sponsors and hosts a reality TV
show called "The Cut", in which
the winner is given the opportunity
to design for Tommy Hilfiger

55
Taken private by Apax Partners for
US$1.6 billion, opening up the potential
for the brand in the European market

57
Marries his second
wife, fashion designer
Dee Ocleppo

$ **$3 BILLION**

PVH ← TOMMY HILFIGER

project RUNWAY

59
Sells company to Phillips-Van
Heusen for US$3 billion

58
Becomes a guest judge on an episode
of the reality TV show "Project Runway"

SEE NOW BUY NOW

65
Collaborates with model Gigi Hadid on the first of 4
collections. Within the first 48 hours of the launch,
the brand's website traffic increases by 900%

Becomes the first American designer to test the
"see-now-buy-now" system, with customers able
to shop directly after the show

JEAN PAUL GAULTIER

DATE OF BIRTH
24 April 1952

BIRTHPLACE
France

LABEL
Pierre Cardin, Jean Paul Gaultier,
Hermès

"I would like to say to people, open your eyes and find beauty where you normally don't expect it."

1952 → 0
Born in Val-de-Marne, France

Makes a conical bra for Nana

13
Designs a collection for his
mother and grandmother

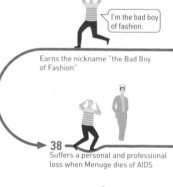

I'm the bad boy of fashion.

Earns the nickname "the Bad Boy
of Fashion"

38
Suffers a personal and professional
loss when Menuge dies of AIDS

57
Collaborates with Target on
an affordable clothing line

54
Includes plus-size models
in his show

Launches a makeup line for men:
Tout Beau, Tout Propre

Bye!

HERMÈS
PARIS

58
Ends his relationship with Hermès
and presents SS11 as his last show

59
Stages his first international retrospective,
"The Fashion World of Jean Paul Gaultier:
From the Sidewalk to the Catwalk"

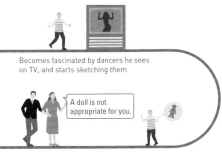

Becomes fascinated by dancers he sees on TV, and starts sketching them

A doll is not appropriate for you.

Asks his parents for a doll, but is given a teddy bear he names Nana

⟶ CAREER HIGHLIGHTS ⟶

Affectionately nicknamed *l'enfant terrible* as a child due to his rebellious streak, Gaultier realized his interest in fashion from a young age. Challenging the traditional notions of fashion with vibrant collections and outrageous shows, Gaultier created a name for himself as a provocative fashion force, playing with sexuality and gender, embracing different shapes, sizes, and ages, and creating iconic designs, including Madonna's famous conical bras.

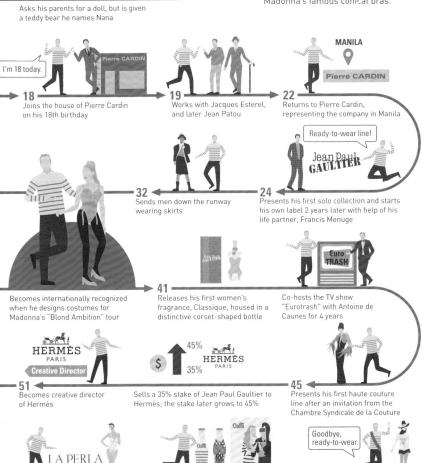

I'm 18 today.

18
Joins the house of Pierre Cardin on his 18th birthday

19
Works with Jacques Esterel, and later Jean Patou

MANILA
Pierre CARDIN

22
Returns to Pierre Cardin, representing the company in Manila

Ready-to-wear line!

Jean Paul GAULTIER

32
Sends men down the runway wearing skirts

24
Presents his first solo collection and starts his own label 2 years later with help of his life partner, Francis Menuge

Becomes internationally recognized when he designs costumes for Madonna's "Blond Ambition" tour

41
Releases his first women's fragrance, Classique, housed in a distinctive corset-shaped bottle

Euro TRASH

Co-hosts the TV show "Eurotrash" with Antoine de Caunes for 4 years

HERMÈS
PARIS
Creative Director

51
Becomes creative director of Hermès

45%
$
35%
HERMÈS
PARIS

Sells a 35% stake of Jean Paul Gaultier to Hermès; the stake later grows to 45%

45
Presents his first haute couture line after an invitation from the Chambre Syndicale de la Couture

LA PERLA

Debuts his first swimwear collection in collaboration with La Perla

60
Becomes Diet Coke's new creative director

Goodbye, ready-to-wear.

62
Announces the closure of his ready-to-wear label to focus on haute couture

HELMUT LANG

DATE OF BIRTH
10 March 1956

BIRTHPLACE
Austria

LABEL
Helmut Lang

— CAREER HIGHLIGHTS —

Lang approached fashion design like an artist, but at the same time kept clothes wearable. Never intending to become a famous fashion designer, he quietly rose to cult status by creating influential minimalist designs and innovative presentations, including staging men's and women's shows together and shifting New York Fashion Week's schedule. Lang retired from fashion in 2005, but his influence is evident in many designers' work to this day.

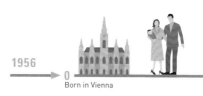

1956

0
Born in Vienna

23
Opens a made-to-measure shop, Bou Bou Lang, in Vienna, with just 3 members of staff

Internet-based show!

Cancels his runway presentation and shows collection images online, creating the first-ever internet-based show

43
Introduces the Astro Moto jacket and backpack-style internal straps on coats in his AW99 astronaut- and biker-inspired collection

44
Advertises in *National Geographic* instead of a fashion magazine

You've lost your edge.

Journalists comment that Lang has lost his edge since Prada gained control of his brand

Plans to show in Paris, but changes his mind after the 9/11 attacks, staying in New York and continuing to show on the internet

46
Moves the presentation of his collections back to Paris

$100 MILLION
▼
$37 MILLION

47
Sales fall from over US$100 million in 1999 to US$37 million

His parents divorce and send him to live with his grandparents in the Austrian Alps

Helps his grandfather in his shoemaking workshop, mending and stitching leather mountain boots

HELMUT LANG

21

Launches his eponymous label

Bye, Dad.

18

Moves out of his father's house and begins to design clothing for himself

> I had a classic bad stepmother – like in a Hollywood movie.

10

His father remarries and brings Lang back to Vienna to live with him and his wife

28

Closes his shop, and presents a women's collection at the Centre Pompidou in Paris 2 years later

37

Appointed professor of fashion design at the University of Applied Arts, Vienna

41

Becomes one of the first designers to show menswear and womenswear simultaneously

New York first.

Moves up the date of his SS99 show, prompting other designers to follow suit; this results in New York becoming the first city on the global Fashion Week roster

HELMUT LANG

42

Relocates his company from Vienna to New York, becoming the first fashion house to make a transcontinental move

DECADE'S MOST INFLUENTIAL DESIGNERS

Recognized by the fashion press as one of the decade's most influential designers

51% **PRADA**

HELMUT LANG

Sells a 51% stake of his company to the Prada Group, controlling only the brand's design and advertising

> "I was never so directly inspired by fashion. It always came from somewhere else."

100% **PRADA**

HELMUT LANG

48

Sells his entire business to Prada

Bye.

49

Presents his last show and retires from the fashion business

55

Shreds the remaining 6,000 garments from his archive after a large portion of it is damaged in a fire; creates the installation "Make It Hard"

MARTIN MARGIELA

DATE OF BIRTH
9 April 1957

BIRTHPLACE
Belgium

LABEL
Maison Martin Margiela, Hermès

1957 → **0**
Born in Genk, Belgium

27
Moves to Paris and works as a design assistant for Jean Paul Gaultier

30
Rei Kawakubo orders Margiela's split-toe Tabi shoes after seeing Meirens wearing a complete Margiela outfit

40
Presents a new white, rectangular garment label with circled black numbers indicating different lines

38
Presents his AW95 collection, once again using masked models – a move he continues to make throughout his collections

HERMÈS
PARIS
Creative Director

Appointed creative director of the Hermès womenswear line

41
Uses men in white lab coats holding garments on hangers to present his SS98 collection

45
Sells the Margiela brand to the parent company of Diesel, Renzo Rosso's OTB Group

51
Retrospective exhibition takes place at the Antwerp Mode Museum; it then travels to Munich

49
Invited by the Chambre Syndicale to show his first haute couture collection, Maison Margiela Artisanal, on the official Paris schedule

Goodbye...

Maison Martin Margiela
PARIS

52
Quietly resigns from his role as creative director of his own line, and disappears from the fashion industry

60
Stages an exhibition at the Mode Museum in Antwerp called "Margiela: The Hermès Years"

Contributes to a retrospective at the Parisian fashion museum Palais Galliera

I want to be a fashion designer...

Aspires to be a fashion designer after seeing a news story about Paco Rabanne and André Courrèges on TV

18
Moves to Antwerp to study fashion at the Royal Academy of Fine Arts

Judge

Entrant

26
Meets Jenny Meirens, the owner of a Brussels boutique, at the Golden Spindle awards ceremony, where he is an entrant and she is a judge

23
Works as a freelance designer for more than 5 years

Maison Martin Margiela
PARIS

31
Founds Maison Martin Margiela in Paris, in partnership with Meirens

Presents the first Maison Martin Margiela collection, SS89, with masked models showcasing the now-iconic Tabi boots

37
Debuts his AIDS awareness T-shirt for charity; it later becomes a collectors' item

CLASSIFIED

Maison Martin Margiela A/W 89

Advertises the invitation to his AW89 show in the classifieds section of a newspaper

ANDAM
FASHION AWARD
PARIS

32
Becomes the first person to receive the ANDAM Award, a prestigious fashion accolade

I'm stepping down...

46
Steps down from his role at Hermès, with his former boss Jean Paul Gaultier taking over

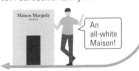

Maison Margiela
PARIS

An all-white Maison!

47
Moves to new headquarters, a former orphanage that had been empty for 10 years, and repaints the entire 3,000-square-foot space white

61
Collaborates on a film called "Martin Margiela: In His Own Words". It is the first official documentary about the designer's career

"I react against everything that's chic and traditional. If you don't revolt, then you don't go anywhere."

—— **CAREER HIGHLIGHTS** ——

Preferring to stay out of the public eye, Margiela managed to maintain an air of mystery throughout his career. Considered one of the most influential designers of the 21st century, he challenged the fashion world and brought a fresh and evolving perspective to the industry. He kept fans and fashion insiders alike guessing by staging shows in unexpected places, casting models off the street, and applying skilled tailoring to cheap materials.

DRIES VAN NOTEN

DATE OF BIRTH
12 May 1958

BIRTHPLACE
Belgium

LABEL
Dries Van Noten

— CAREER HIGHLIGHTS —

Van Noten was part of the legendary gang of designers that formed the Antwerp Six in the 1980s and 90s. The designer impressively forged a business, then an empire, without external investment or ad campaigns. Although he was the third generation of his family to work in fashion, he did not follow a traditional path. Instead, he made a name for himself as one of the most sought-after designers in the world thanks to his unique color palette and unusual fabric choices.

1958

0
Born in Antwerp, Belgium, into a family of tailors

The collection enjoys immediate success; his first order comes from Barneys New York

Opens a tiny boutique in Antwerp's gallery arcade

29
Presents his first women's collection

INDIA My inspiration!

Meets his business partner, Christine Mathys, and travels to India, which later becomes his main source of inspiration

33
Stages his first menswear show in Paris

53
Creates costumes for contemporary ballet "Rain" by choreographer Anne Teresa de Keersmaeker

48
Adopts a modern and less folk-inspired aesthetic for his SS07 collection

56
Showcases his designs and influences in an exhibition called "Inspirations" at the Musée des Arts Décoratifs in Paris

58
Becomes the first designer to hold a show in the Grand Opera Palais Garnier, home of the Paris Opera

HONORARY TITLE OF BARON

59
Receives the honorary title of baron, the most important and highest Belgian award

Follows his father to menswear shows and learns about the commercial and technical aspects of fashion

18

Studies fashion design at Antwerp's Royal Academy and begins freelancing as a designer

Showcases his first menswear collection in London, along with 5 schoolmates, in order to share the cost; they are dubbed the Antwerp Six

28

Sets up his namesake label, promising to make only ready-to-wear

31

Meets his creative and life partner, Patrick Vangheluwe

> "Our role is to dream and inspire rather than collude in impacting the reality."

Swaps his modest boutique for a 5-story historical building – a former department store that once housed his grandfather's greatest competitors

36

Creates his first womenswear show, Flower; it is the first time he uses prints, and it is a commercial success

41

Undergoes a difficult transition after Mathys dies

46

Celebrates his 50th fashion show with a 500-person dinner; the table becomes the catwalk for his womenswear presentation

42

Moves his headquarters to a 60,000-square-foot warehouse; the top floor has breathtaking views across the city

Makes the documentary "Dries"; it is the first time he allows a filmmaker to accompany him during his creative process

Pays homage to models and muses of all ages at his 100th show

60

Sells a majority stake in his brand to Puig after being independent for more than 30 years

DOMENICO DOLCE

DOMENICO MARIO
ASSUNTO DOLCE

DATE OF BIRTH
13 August 1958

BIRTHPLACE
Italy

LABEL
Dolce & Gabbana

STEFANO GABBANA

DATE OF BIRTH
14 November 1962

BIRTHPLACE
Italy

LABEL
Dolce & Gabbana

"I'm lucky because I met Domenico in my life – and I think he's lucky to have met me too." – Stefano Gabbana

1958

0
Domenico Dolce is born in Sicily, to a father who is a tailor

1962

0
Stefano Gabbana is born in Milan, to a father who works in printing factories

D:27
S:23
They show their first collection at Milan's New Talents fashion show

D:35
S:31
The label courts global fame after designing 1,500 costumes for Madonna's "Girlie Show" world tour

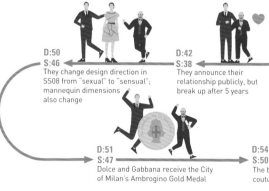

D:50
S:46
They change design direction in SS08 from "sexual" to "sensual"; mannequin dimensions also change

D:42
S:38
They announce their relationship publicly, but break up after 5 years

D:40
S:36
The label secures reliable production by signing an agreement with a clothing firm owned by Dolce's family

D:51
S:47
Dolce and Gabbana receive the City of Milan's Ambrogino Gold Medal

D:54
S:50
The brand launches its first couture show in Taormina, Sicily

Studies at Istituto Marangoni in Milan, but drops out early

Advertising

GRAPHIC DESIGN

Studies graphic design at university

Hi!

D:22
S:18
Dolce answers Gabbana's job-inquiry call

Dolce becomes Gabbana's mentor and teaches him how to sketch and design

DOLCE & GABBANA

D:24
S:20
The duo shares an apartment after Gabbana returns, and they work together relentlessly on the launch of Dolce & Gabbana

Gabbana is called up for 18 months of mandatory military service

D:28
S:24
The duo receives a lot of press coverage, with their sexy designs standing out during the power-dressing era

My family can help with production!

The label is rescued by Dolce's family, who produce their second collection for them when their manufacturer suddenly pulls out

We're too Italian for Italians!

The brand receives interest and appreciation from British and American buyers before Italian buyers catch on

Dolce finally compromises and infuses Sicilian style into the brand, which is later globally recognized as the style of Dolce & Gabbana

They enlist friends to model their second collection, starting the trend of not only using traditional models in their advertising

D&G
DOLCE E GABBANA

D:36
S:32
Introduces the more affordable diffusion line D&G, which closes in 2011

We can retire next year!

SALES

D:39
S:35
Dolce & Gabbana reports a turnover of US$400 million, prompting them to joke about retirement

—— CAREER HIGHLIGHTS ——

The Italian darling duo Dolce and Gabbana have completely different characters, but always bring out the best in each other. With Dolce focused on craftsmanship and Gabbana on looks, the pair is considered one of the world's most successful design partnerships. Often inspired by Mediterranean style, they offer a new point of view every season, playing with countries and historical eras, and experimenting with refreshing, eclectic styles and fabrics.

Overturn the conviction!

TAX EVASION

D:56
S:52
They successfully appeal to overturn their conviction of tax evasion

D:60
S:56
The duo releases controversial videos for their runway event in Shanghai, resulting in models pulling out, and the eventual cancellation of the show

We apologize.

Not Me

Gabbana claims that his account was hacked when racist Instagram DMs leak, leading to Chinese retailers dropping the brand

MICHAEL KORS
MICHAEL DAVID KORS / KARL ANDERSON JR.

DATE OF BIRTH
9 August 1959

BIRTHPLACE
United States of America

LABELS
Michael Kors, Céline

— CAREER HIGHLIGHTS —

With a knack for adapting his business to align with the needs of his customers, Kors created an empire. Knowing his goals from an early age, Kors' energetic and optimistic character helped him navigate the curves in the road, allowing him to successfully become a designer known for chic sportswear and affordable luxury.

1959

0
Born in Long Island, New York

I don't want to be a model...

14
Gives up modeling and acting to pursue a career in design

I work at Lothar's!

18
Enrolls at the Fashion Institute of Technology but drops out after 9 months to accept a position at Manhattan boutique Lothar's

KORS
MICHAEL KORS

31
Launches KORS Michael Kors as a licensee, but puts it on hold after the closure of the llicensee partner

34
Files for bankruptcy due to the closure of his licensing partner

MICHAEL KORS

45
Opens his first retail store, 25 years after the creation of the label

MICHAEL
MICHAEL KORS

Launches a less expensive diffusion line, MICHAEL Michael Kors

50
Receives attention when First Lady Michelle Obama wears one of his designs for the first official White House portrait, as well as at other occasions

LIFETIME ACHIEVEMENT AWARD

51
Becomes the youngest recipient of the CFDA Geoffrey Beene Lifetime Achievement Award

52
Marries partner Lance Le Pere

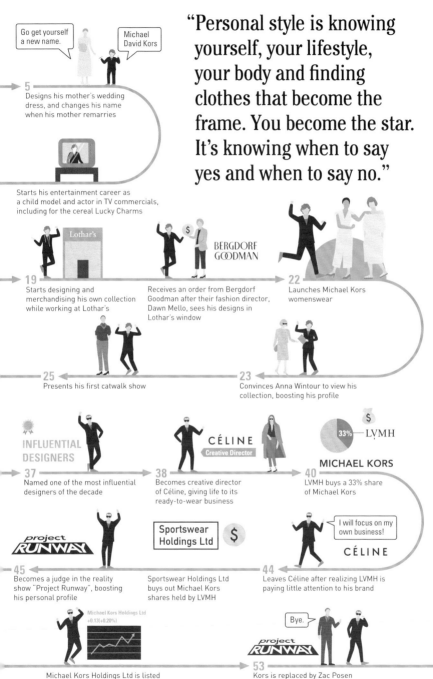

"Personal style is knowing yourself, your lifestyle, your body and finding clothes that become the frame. You become the star. It's knowing when to say yes and when to say no."

Go get yourself a new name.

Michael David Kors

5
Designs his mother's wedding dress, and changes his name when his mother remarries

Starts his entertainment career as a child model and actor in TV commercials, including for the cereal Lucky Charms

Lothar's

19
Starts designing and merchandising his own collection while working at Lothar's

$

BERGDORF GOODMAN

22
Launches Michael Kors womenswear

Receives an order from Bergdorf Goodman after their fashion director, Dawn Mello, sees his designs in Lothar's window

25
Presents his first catwalk show

23
Convinces Anna Wintour to view his collection, boosting his profile

INFLUENTIAL DESIGNERS

CÉLINE
Creative Director

33% — LVMH

MICHAEL KORS

37
Named one of the most influential designers of the decade

38
Becomes creative director of Céline, giving life to its ready-to-wear business

40
LVMH buys a 33% share of Michael Kors

project RUNWAY

Sportswear Holdings Ltd

$

I will focus on my own business!

CÉLINE

45
Becomes a judge in the reality show "Project Runway", boosting his personal profile

Sportswear Holdings Ltd buys out Michael Kors shares held by LVMH

44
Leaves Céline after realizing LVMH is paying little attention to his brand

Michael Kors Holdings Ltd +0.13(+0.20%)

Bye.

project RUNWAY

Michael Kors Holdings Ltd is listed on the New York Stock Exchange

53
Kors is replaced by Zac Posen on "Project Runway"

ANN DEMEULEMEESTER

DATE OF BIRTH
29 December 1959

BIRTHPLACE
Belgium

LABEL
Ann Demeulemeester

> "For me, black is not dark, it's poetic. I don't think of gothic, I think of classic — it's a big difference."

1959

0
Born in Waregem, Belgium to a history-professor father

The idea that garments are alive is a big inspiration. I want to fill them with soul.

Fascinated by how people are characterized by their clothing, she starts drawing portraits

I have to know this person.

Becomes obsessed with Patti Smith, the godmother of punk, after discovering her album "Horses"

26
Launches her clothing line with her photographer husband, Patrick Robyn

27
Showcases rebellious, avant-garde collections in London along with other 5 schoolmates; they are dubbed the "Antwerp Six"

28
Presents her first women's collection, Light in Paris

Men and women are together.

37
Debuts a menswear collection at her womenswear show

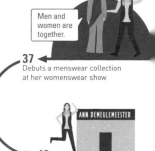

40
Opens her first shop, in Antwerp

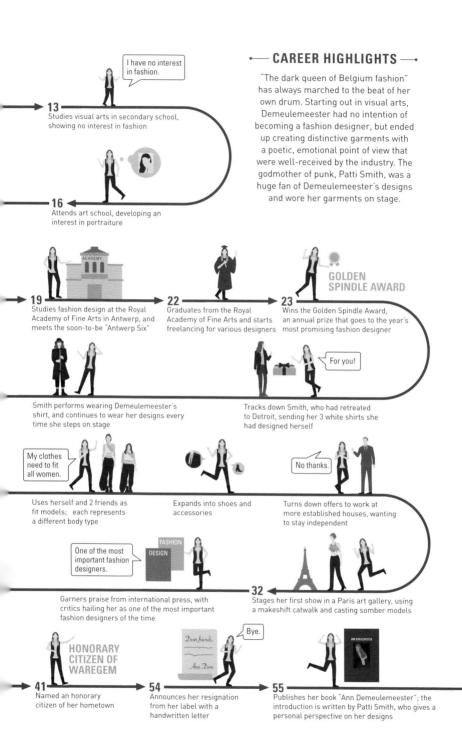

13
Studies visual arts in secondary school, showing no interest in fashion

"I have no interest in fashion."

16
Attends art school, developing an interest in portraiture

"The dark queen of Belgium fashion" has always marched to the beat of her own drum. Starting out in visual arts, Demeulemeester had no intention of becoming a fashion designer, but ended up creating distinctive garments with a poetic, emotional point of view that were well-received by the industry. The godmother of punk, Patti Smith, was a huge fan of Demeulemeester's designs and wore her garments on stage.

19
Studies fashion design at the Royal Academy of Fine Arts in Antwerp, and meets the soon-to-be "Antwerp Six"

22
Graduates from the Royal Academy of Fine Arts and starts freelancing for various designers

23
Wins the Golden Spindle Award, an annual prize that goes to the year's most promising fashion designer

GOLDEN SPINDLE AWARD

Smith performs wearing Demeulemeester's shirt, and continues to wear her designs every time she steps on stage

"For you!"

Tracks down Smith, who had retreated to Detroit, sending her 3 white shirts she had designed herself

"My clothes need to fit all women."

Uses herself and 2 friends as fit models; each represents a different body type

Expands into shoes and accessories

"No thanks."

Turns down offers to work at more established houses, wanting to stay independent

"One of the most important fashion designers."

FASHION DESIGN

Garners praise from international press, with critics hailing her as one of the most important fashion designers of the time

32
Stages her first show in a Paris art gallery, using a makeshift catwalk and casting somber models

HONORARY CITIZEN OF WAREGEM

41
Named an honorary citizen of her hometown

Dear friends,

Ann Dem

"Bye."

54
Announces her resignation from her label with a handwritten letter

ANN DEMEULEMEESTER

55
Publishes her book "Ann Demeulemeester"; the introduction is written by Patti Smith, who gives a personal perspective on her designs

ICONIC ITEMS
BY DESIGNERS BORN DURING THE 1950s

1 TEDDY BEAR COAT & HAT – FRANCO MOSCHINO

Introduced in 1988
Mocking expensive fur coats, Moschino made headlines by decorating a classically cut coat with a collar of teddy bears. A pioneer in rejecting real fur in fashion – making a faux-fur collection called Fun Fur in AW89 – Moschino aimed to highlight the ludicrousness of draping yourself in a dead animals.

2 CONICAL BRA – JEAN PAUL GAULTIER

Introduced in 1984
Madonna marked a moment in fashion history when she performed in a pink cone-bra corset. The daring, provocative outfit was inspired by both 1950s bullet bras and the 1980s trend of wearing underwear as outerwear – a style first seen on the catwalk at Jean Paul Gaultier.

3 ASTRO BIKER JEANS – HELMUT LANG

Introduced in 1999
Inspired by NASA designs, Lang's Astro Biker Jeans were part of his Séance de Travail collection. The look became his trademark, and is popular and iconic to this day.

4

TABI SHOES –
MARTIN MARGIELA

Introduced in 1988
First shown at Maison Margiela's debut show in 1988, Tabi shoes are a reinterpretation of the traditional Japanese split-toe sock. During the show, Margiela drenched his models in red paint, so the distinctive hoof-like footprint remained imprinted on the white catwalk.

5

ANDROGYNOUS LOOK –
ANN DEMEULEMEESTER

Introduced in 1992
One of the first designers to merge womenswear and menswear, Demeulemeester redefined the notion of gender with her unisex tailoring and silhouettes. Her pioneering styles were showcased early in her career.

6

LOGO TEE –
TOMMY HILFIGER

Introduced in 1994
Rapper Snoop Dogg wore a signature red, white, and blue Hilfiger rugby shirt for an appearance on a 1994 episode of "Saturday Night Live". New York stores quickly sold out of the style, and Hilfiger sportswear became a highly sought-after commodity among young people.

BORN DURING OR AFTER THE

1960s

Thanks to the rise of fast fashion and a global mash-up of influences, designers born during and after the 1960s are perhaps more versatile, flexible and adaptive than those of previous generations. Their chameleon-like nature allows them to jump between different positions at multiple brands, presenting contrasting ideas and aesthetics at each one. There is also a shift in how designers achieve success: no longer is it necessary for them to have their own label. Many have reached superstar status at the helm of existing luxury houses.

JOHN GALLIANO
JUAN CARLOS ANTONIO GALLIANO-GUILLÉN

DATE OF BIRTH
28 November 1960

BIRTHPLACE
Gibraltar

LABELS
Givenchy, Dior, John Galliano, Maison Margiela

1960

0
Born in Gibraltar to a Spanish mother and Gibraltarian father

20
Enrolls at Central Saint Martins College of Art and Design

Works as a dresser at the National Theatre

Now I can show in Paris.

30
Makes his Paris runway debut with support from Tangiers-born French designer Fayçal Amor

29
Files for bankruptcy and moves to Paris in search of financial backing to save his company

33
Forced to miss a season when his financial agreement with Amor ends

Introduced by Anna Wintour to banker John Bult and fashion patron São Schlumberger, who provide financial backing

I am guilty...

50
Found guilty of making racist insults and anti-Semitic remarks to a fellow customer at a café in Paris

49
Receives the rank of Knight of the Legion of Honor, the highest civilian order in France, but the rank is withdrawn in 2012

Suffers when his right-hand man, Steven Robinson, dies at the age of 38

Come help me.

John Galliano
Christian Dior   LVMH

51
Dismissed from John Galliano and Dior by LVMH

53
Helps Oscar de la Renta prepare for his show through a referral from Anna Wintour

"You only get a short life, so take chances."

6
Moves to London with his family

UNDISTINGUISHED STUDENT

16
Regarded as an undistinguished student for his shy, withdrawn personality

CAREER HIGHLIGHTS

Galliano found success early in his career, making waves with his theatrical graduation show and garnering interest from international buyers. However, after anti-Semitic remarks leaked, the designer was forced to retreat from the spotlight. Almost 3 years later, he came back onto the fashion scene invigorated and with a new project.

"Les Incroyables", inspired by the French Revolution.

24
His graduate collection, inspired by the French Revolution, is bought in its entirety by British boutique Browns

John Galliano

Launches his own label, collaborating with stylist Amanda Harlech and milliner Stephen Jones

Feels a tremendous amount of pressure and spends his money on partying and an excessive lifestyle

$ LVMH

Creative Director
GIVENCHY

35
Appointed creative director at Givenchy

Christian Dior

36
Moves from Givenchy to Christian Dior; LVMH buys Galliano's company

Creates 17 looks in 3 weeks to meet the February shows

60th anniversary of Dior.

47
Presents a breathtaking couture show to mark the 60th anniversary of Dior

37
Presents his first couture collection for Dior on the 50th anniversary of the New Look; it is hailed as a dazzling triumph

My new look.

Maison Margiela
PARIS

54
Joins Maison Margiela as creative director, marking the designer's return to fashion

55
Exhibits first couture collection for Maison Margiela

ALBER ELBAZ

DATE OF BIRTH
12 June 1961

BIRTHPLACE
Morocco

LABELS
Guy Laroche, Yves Saint Laurent,
Lanvin

—— CAREER HIGHLIGHTS ——

Elbaz had his own design rules. He
fantasized about being thin, and used that
desire to bring lightness to his designs.
In his 14 years at the creative helm of
Lanvin, the company became one of the
most coveted brands in the world. Given
freedom in his role, he was able to put his
heart and soul into his creations,
and always strove to bring the best
he could to the brand.

1961

0
Born in Casablanca to a painter mother
and hair-colorist father

28
Works for Geoffrey Beene for 7 years and
is strongly influenced by Beene's design
philosophy and draping skills

LANVIN
Creative Director

40
Becomes creative director of Lanvin

44
Introduces new packaging for Lanvin in a shade
of blue that the label's founder, Jeanne Lanvin,
reportedly saw in frescoes by Fra Angelico

51
Tells the *Wall Street Journal* that he can create
lightness in his designs even though he is overweight

49
Designs an affordable Lanvin
collection for high-street retailer H&M

52
Launches a limited-
edition makeup line for
Lancôme featuring his
illustrations

54
Designs costumes for Natalie
Portman in the film "A Tale of
Love and Darkness"

Announces his departure from
Lanvin, after disagreeing with a
major shareholder

7
Sketches what his teacher wears to school every day for an entire year

10
Immigrates to Israel with his family

I'll be in charge of entertainment.

18
Starts mandatory service in the Israeli Army, and is placed in charge of entertainment, for health reasons

25
Encouraged by his mother to move to New York and pursue a career in fashion

21
Toys with the idea of pursuing an acting career, but ends up studying fashion design at the Shenkar College of Engineering, Design and Art in Israel

32
Meets partner Alex Koo

1996
Guy Laroche Paris
Parfums
Creative Director

1998
YSL
Head designer

35
Becomes creative director of couture house Guy Laroche; 2 years later becomes head designer at Yves Saint Laurent

This isn't working out.

KRIZIA

Works for Krizia in Italy, but leaves after 3 months, reportedly due to a dispute with the label's founder

Bye. GUCCI $ → YSL

38
Is replaced by Tom Ford when Gucci buys Yves Saint Laurent

48
Receives the city's highest distinction, the Medal of the City of Paris, from Mayor Bertrand Delanoë

Creates 2 stamp designs for France's postal service in celebration of Lanvin's 120th anniversary

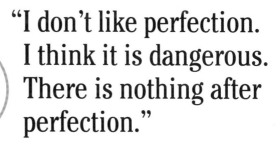

"I don't like perfection. I think it is dangerous. There is nothing after perfection."

ALL★STAR ALBER

55
Collaborates with Converse on a high-end collection called Avant Converse

$30 MILLION
AZ FACTORY
RICHEMONT

59
Invests USD$30 million to launch an innovative new brand, AZ Factory, with Richemont

ALBER ELBAZ

59
Dies of COVID-19 in Paris

TOM FORD
THOMAS CARLYLE FORD

DATE OF BIRTH
27 August 1961

BIRTHPLACE
United States of America

LABELS
**Perry Ellis, Gucci,
Yves Saint Laurent, Tom Ford**

1961

0
Born in Austin, Texas

Art History.

18
Studies art history at New York University

Frequents Studio 54, a nightclub favored by A-listers, and earns a living as a model, expanding his contacts in the fashion world

GUCCI
Creative Director

PERRY ELLIS
Design Director

29
Moves to Milan and joins Gucci as a womenswear designer through Dawn Mello, a friend of Buckley's; after 4 years, he is appointed creative director

27
Works as design director at Perry Ellis

GUCCI
Creative Director

34
Presents his SS95 collection; critics consider it Tom Ford's arrival as a designer

38
Becomes creative and communications director of YSL after Gucci Group's takeover

It is too provocative...
We need to ban it.

TOM FORD FOR MEN

A provocative ad for his men's fragrance, shot by Terry Richardson, is banned in several countries

TOM FORD

845 Madison Avenue in New York.

46
Starts his own label, initially focused on menswear; it is only available at one Tom Ford store

A SINGLE MAN

48
Directs his first film, "A Single Man"

Cameras and cell phones are not allowed.

49
Presents a womenswear collection to a limited number of attendees ahead of the general public; there is a strict no-cameras, no-phones policy during the preview

11
Moves to Santa Fe, New Mexico with his family

> # "I probably do have an obsessive personality, but striving for perfection has served me well."

Ford started out trying to be an actor in Hollywood, but found his true calling when he switched to fashion design. An exceptional salesman, Ford has a knack for creating glamorous yet commercial designs. His clear vision was credited with reviving Gucci from near bankruptcy; he then went on to launch his eponymous label, which has successfully expanded into the beauty arena. Conquering the fashion and beauty worlds with his perfectionist's eye, Ford moved into film directing, discovering yet another talent.

12
Learns the importance of good dress sense from his grandmother, and receives his first pair of Gucci loafers

21
Drops out of New York University and studies architecture at Parsons School of Design, later switching to the Paris branch of the college

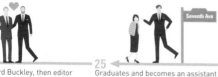

Meets Richard Buckley, then editor of *Women's Wear Daily*; they become life partners

25
Graduates and becomes an assistant to designer Cathy Hardwick

Takes a year off to work as an intern in the press office of Chloé in Paris

Yves Saint Laurent speaks openly about his displeasure with Tom Ford and his work at YSL

43
Shows his final Gucci collection, increasing the house's revenue from US$200 million to US$2.5 billion

44
Partners with the Marcolin Group to produce and distribute eyewear under his name

Announces the launch of his film production company, Fade to Black

Launches Tom Ford Beauty in partnership with Estée Lauder; the brand redefines luxury beauty

51
His son with Richard Buckley, Alexander John Buckley Ford, is born; the couple marries 2 years later

56
Becomes one of few designers to adopt the see-now-buy-now fashion model, but soon drops it

MARC JACOBS

DATE OF BIRTH
9 April 1963

BIRTHPLACE
United States of America

LABELS
Marc Jacobs, Louis Vuitton

"I always find beauty in things that are odd and imperfect – they are much more interesting."

— CAREER HIGHLIGHTS —

An adolescence spent living with his grandmother, who encouraged self-expression, helped turn Jacobs into a free spirit. While the designer's life has not been without its struggles – Jacobs almost went bankrupt, and has dealt with substance-abuse issues – he has left an impressive footprint on the fashion industry. Not only did he inject a modern point of view into French fashion house Louis Vuitton, he has also presented quirky and offbeat styles through his main and diffusion lines.

1963

0
Born in New York; his parents are talent agents

24
Is greatly affected by the death of his grandmother

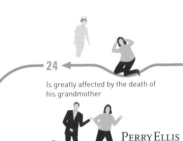

PERRY ELLIS

25
Takes over the womenswear division of Perry Ellis with Duffy

MARC BY MARC JACOBS

38
Introduces a more affordable diffusion line, Marc by Marc Jacobs, which runs until 2015

Collaborates with artist Takashi Murakami on a range of bags for Louis Vuitton, revitalizing the historic house

BANG

47
Poses naked in the ad campaign for his new men's fragrance, Bang

MEMBER OF THE CFDA BOARD OF DIRECTORS

48
Becomes a member of the CFDA board of directors

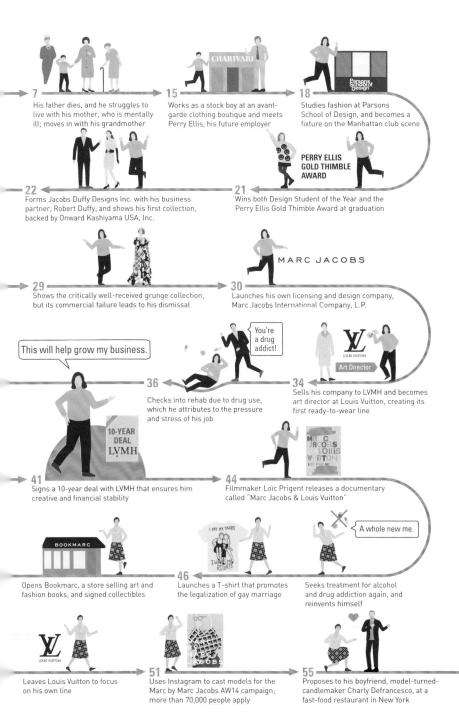

7
His father dies, and he struggles to live with his mother, who is mentally ill; moves in with his grandmother

15
Works as a stock boy at an avant-garde clothing boutique and meets Perry Ellis, his future employer

18
Studies fashion at Parsons School of Design, and becomes a fixture on the Manhattan club scene

PERRY ELLIS GOLD THIMBLE AWARD

22
Forms Jacobs Duffy Designs Inc. with his business partner, Robert Duffy, and shows his first collection, backed by Onward Kashiyama USA, Inc.

21
Wins both Design Student of the Year and the Perry Ellis Gold Thimble Award at graduation

29
Shows the critically well-received grunge collection, but its commercial failure leads to his dismissal

30
Launches his own licensing and design company, Marc Jacobs International Company, L.P.

MARC JACOBS

You're a drug addict!

This will help grow my business.

36
Checks into rehab due to drug use, which he attributes to the pressure and stress of his job

34
Sells his company to LVMH and becomes art director at Louis Vuitton, creating its first ready-to-wear line

Art Director

10-YEAR DEAL LVMH

41
Signs a 10-year deal with LVMH that ensures him creative and financial stability

44
Filmmaker Loïc Prigent releases a documentary called "Marc Jacobs & Louis Vuitton"

A whole new me.

BOOKMARC

Opens Bookmarc, a store selling art and fashion books, and signed collectibles

46
Launches a T-shirt that promotes the legalization of gay marriage

Seeks treatment for alcohol and drug addiction again, and reinvents himself

Leaves Louis Vuitton to focus on his own line

51
Uses Instagram to cast models for the Marc by Marc Jacobs AW14 campaign; more than 70,000 people apply

55
Proposes to his boyfriend, model-turned-candlemaker Charly Defrancesco, at a fast-food restaurant in New York

THOM BROWNE
THOMAS BROWNE

DATE OF BIRTH
19 April 1965

BIRTHPLACE
United States of America

LABEL
Thom Browne

1965 → **0**
Born in Allentown, Pennsylvania

33
Invited by Ralph Lauren to become
a designer for Club Monaco

Develops his main source of sartorial
inspiration from his father

I can't afford a catwalk, so I'll try the sidewalk.

In a form of guerrilla advertising, he creates 5 suits for
himself and wears them around town trying to get noticed,
as he is unable to fund a full collection

Draws inspiration from classic mid-20th-century American style
and mixes it with preppy details, honing his signature aesthetic

38
Debuts his first line of ready-to-wear
menswear

Collaborates with Moncler on a range called
Gamme Bleu

44
Collaborates with Harry Winston on a jewelry line

46
Designs his first full women's
ready-to-wear line

Begins a relationship with Andrew Bolton,
head curator of the Metropolitan Museum of
Art's Costume Institute; Bolton is also a fan of
Browne's designs

Studies business at the University of Notre Dame

I am a financial consultant.

Becomes a financial consultant after graduation, but the career lasts less than a year

I'll try my hand at fashion.

I'll be the only Thom Browne.

32

Moves to New York to pursue a fashion career

Discovers a passion for altering vintage men's tailoring with Johnson Hartig, who later co-founds Libertine

23

Moves to Hollywood to pursue his dream of becoming an actor, and changes his name to Thom after finding out that there is already a Tom Browne in the Screen Actors Guild

Check me out!

36

Launches a line of made-to-measure menswear, with a focus on shrunken proportions that become his signature

"It is so important to be really true to yourself in design, and I am."

Brooks Brothers
ESTABLISHED 1818

42

Collaborates with Brooks Brothers on a high-end collection called Black Fleece

CAREER HIGHLIGHTS

A master of modern tailoring, Browne started his career from humble beginnings. He ran every aspect of his business himself, and followed a clear set of tasks, day in, day out, to achieve his goals. And achieve he did, by introducing a new "shrunken" approach to tailoring that saw tremendous success, and redefining the way men wear suits.

It's my dog Hector.

48

Receives wide recognition when First Lady Michelle Obama wears his designs to the inauguration

51

Features his dog, Hector Browne, in his collection, designing a bag inspired by him

RAF SIMONS
RAF JAN SIMONS

DATE OF BIRTH
12 January 1968

BIRTHPLACE
Belgium

LABELS
Raf Simons, Jil Sander,
Christian Dior, Calvin Klein

"I don't want to show clothes, I want to show my attitude, my past, present, and future."

1968

0
Born in Neerpelt, Belgium, to an army night-watchman father and a house-cleaner mother

I want to be a fashion designer!

22
Attends Martin Margiela's show with Beirendonck and is blown away

23
Meets stylist Olivier Rizzo and director Willy Vanderperre, who remain his closest collaborators to this day

35
For SS03, he turns to English graphic designer Peter Saville, and presents parkas printed with Joy Division and New Order album-cover art

RAF
BY RAF SIMONS

37
Launches an affordable diffusion line, Raf by Raf Simons

45
Collaborates with Adidas on a collection that becomes an instant hit

IRRESISTIBLE

DIOR AND I

Stars in the documentary "Dior and I", which premieres at the Tribeca Film Festival

46
Collaborates with Ruby again on the AW14 collection, replacing the designer's eponymous collection

Bye!

Christian Dior

GOOGLE'S TOP TRENDING FASHION DESIGNER OF THE YEAR

47
Appears with new boyfriend Jean-Georges d'Orazio, whom he met while working at Dior

Resigns from Christian Dior and becomes Google's top-trending fashion designer of the year

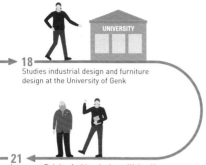

18
Studies industrial design and furniture design at the University of Genk

21
Interns at Belgian fashion designer Walter Van Beirendonck's studio

CAREER HIGHLIGHTS

Initially working in the field of furniture design, Simons switched career paths after watching an awe-inspiring Maison Margiela fashion show. With a knack for reimagining the rules of menswear and blurring the lines between formalwear and sportswear – thanks to clever proportions and the use of graphics – Simons became one of the world's most celebrated designers, and a great influencer of streetwear and men's fashion.

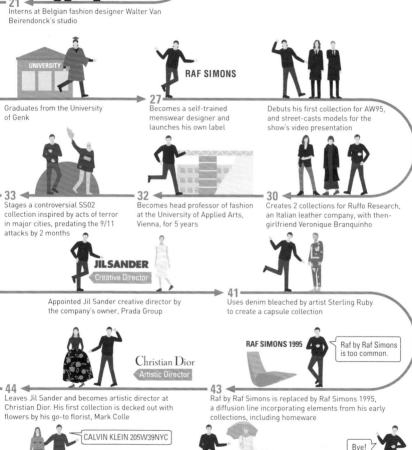

Graduates from the University of Genk

RAF SIMONS

27
Becomes a self-trained menswear designer and launches his own label

Debuts his first collection for AW95, and street-casts models for the show's video presentation

33
Stages a controversial SS02 collection inspired by acts of terror in major cities, predating the 9/11 attacks by 2 months

32
Becomes head professor of fashion at the University of Applied Arts, Vienna, for 5 years

30
Creates 2 collections for Ruffo Research, an Italian leather company, with then-girlfriend Veronique Branquinho

JIL SANDER
Creative Director

Appointed Jil Sander creative director by the company's owner, Prada Group

41
Uses denim bleached by artist Sterling Ruby to create a capsule collection

RAF SIMONS 1995

Raf by Raf Simons is too common.

Christian Dior
Artistic Director

44
Leaves Jil Sander and becomes artistic director at Christian Dior. His first collection is decked out with flowers by his go-to florist, Mark Colle

43
Raf by Raf Simons is replaced by Raf Simons 1995, a diffusion line incorporating elements from his early collections, including homeware

CALVIN KLEIN 205W39NYC

Calvin Klein
Chief Creative Officer

48
Appointed chief creative officer at Calvin Klein, he renames its ready-to-wear collection

Revisits past collections, inspired by Joy Division and his love of Peter Saville's work, for his SS18 show

Bye!

CALVIN KLEIN

50
Parts ways with Calvin Klein after the company decides on a different brand direction

HEDI SLIMANE

DATE OF BIRTH
5 July 1968

BIRTHPLACE
France

LABELS
Dior Homme,
Saint Laurent Paris, Céline

1968

0

Born in the 19th arrondissement of Paris

Bye.

Leaves Yves Saint Laurent after
it is acquired by the Gucci Group

I'll lose weight to
wear your designs!

Dior Homme's business increases by 41%
under Slimane's direction

VISIONAIRE

Guest-edits the quarterly
magazine *Visionaire*

Introduces skinny menswear
for Dior Homme, which
becomes a huge success

Publishes several photography books and, 4 years later,
a personal photography blog, The Diary, featuring rock
stars and unknown cool kids as subjects

Dior

I want to keep
control of my name.

39

Declines to renew his Dior Homme contract
and Dior's offer to fund his own collections, in
order to keep his brand's integrity

45

Uses Dutch artist and model Saskia
de Brauw for his inaugural Saint
Laurent Paris menswear campaign

SAINT LAURENT
PARIS

Changes the label's name
to Saint Laurent Paris and
alters the house's branding

44

Creative Director

Rejoins Yves Saint Laurent as
creative director

The heeled Chelsea boot becomes one of Saint
Laurent Paris' bestselling styles

48

$ 300%

The house's sales triple in
4 years under Slimane's direction

11
Receives his first camera and learns black-and-white darkroom printing

16
Studies art history at École du Louvre and starts making his own clothes

21
Begins a 3-year apprenticeship with menswear designer José Lévy

Menswear Director

31
Introduces a new skinny silhouette in the AW99 Black Tie collection

28
Moves to Yves Saint Laurent as an assistant, soon becoming director of the men's ready-to-wear line

24
Assists fashion consultant Jean-Jacques Picart on a "monogram canvas" project for Louis Vuitton, along with 7 other designers

32
Moves to Berlin on the invitation of curator Klaus Biesenbach; takes up a 2-year residency at the Kunst-Werke Institute for Contemporary Art

DIOR HOMME
Creative Director
JIL SANDER

34
Declines a creative directorship offer at Jil Sander, and accepts a position as creative director for menswear at Christian Dior

Moves to LA and starts photographing the city and its people. Soon his work features in several exhibitions

SWEET BIRD OF YOUTH

Curates his first exhibition, "Sweet Bird of Youth", and a second one, 4 years later, called "California Song"

Bye.
SAINT LAURENT
PARIS

Declines to renew his contract with Saint Laurent Paris, departing over legal issues, including a fight over a US$12 million payment over his non-compete clause

"Fashion somehow, for me, is purely and happily irrational."

CAREER HIGHLIGHTS

Slimane has had a very successful career, driving stellar sales for some of the world's major fashion houses. Not only was his Parisian rock 'n' roll look for Yves Saint Laurent received with critical acclaim; the super-skinny silhouettes he designed for Dior Homme were so popular that even Karl Lagerfeld declared he would lose weight to wear the style. His photography, capturing music and hipster cultures, has only added to his credentials and cool factor.

LVMH
CELINE

49
Announces he is joining Céline (now Celine), part of the LVMH group

ALEXANDER McQUEEN

LEE ALEXANDER McQUEEN

DATE OF BIRTH
17 March 1969

BIRTHPLACE
United Kingdom

LABELS
Alexander McQueen, Givenchy

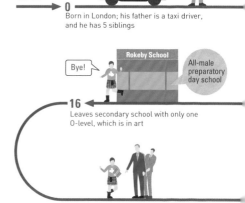

1969
0
Born in London; his father is a taxi driver, and he has 5 siblings

Bye!

Rokeby School

All-male preparatory day school

16
Leaves secondary school with only one O-level, which is in art

Begins an apprenticeship on Savile Row

GIVENCHY
Head Designer

Becomes head designer at Givenchy

27
Designs the wardrobe for David Bowie's tours

29
Features former ballerina Shalom Harlow and 2 industrial robots in his SS99 show

GUCCI 51%
$ $ $

31
The Gucci Group acquires 51% of his company

Marries George Forsyth, but they divorce a year later

"Everyone has a dark side they sometimes try to hide... I guess that makes it more attractive."

SOLD OUT TARGET

39
Creates an affordable line for American department store Target; it quickly sells out

Overdoses on drugs twice

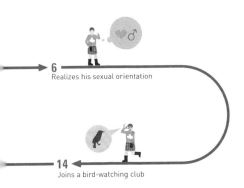

6
Realizes his sexual orientation

14
Joins a bird-watching club

Famous for powerful, shocking – and sometimes even disturbing – shows, McQueen was a bold designer who was not afraid of criticism. Drawing on a broad range of inspirations, from his childhood to politics and nature, his designs blurred the line between fashion and art. His unexpected death left the fashion world in a state of shock and sadness.

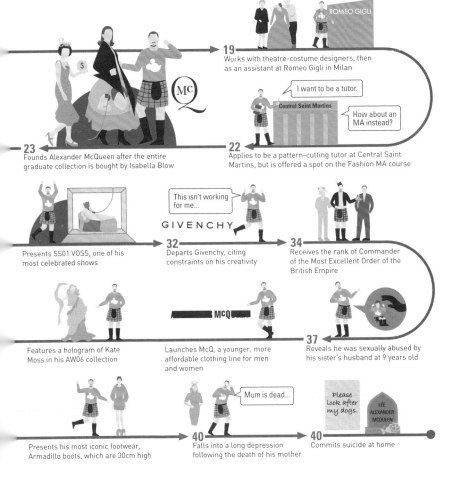

19
Works with theatre-costume designers, then as an assistant at Romeo Gigli in Milan

I want to be a tutor.

How about an MA instead?

Central Saint Martins

22
Applies to be a pattern-cutting tutor at Central Saint Martins, but is offered a spot on the Fashion MA course

23
Founds Alexander McQueen after the entire graduate collection is bought by Isabella Blow

Presents SS01 VOSS, one of his most celebrated shows

This isn't working for me...

GIVENCHY

32
Departs Givenchy, citing constraints on his creativity

34
Receives the rank of Commander of the Most Excellent Order of the British Empire

Features a hologram of Kate Moss in his AW06 collection

MCQ

Launches McQ, a younger, more affordable clothing line for men and women

37
Reveals he was sexually abused by his sister's husband at 9 years old

Presents his most iconic footwear, Armadillo boots, which are 30cm high

Mum is dead...

40
Falls into a long depression following the death of his mother

Please look after my dogs.

LEE ALEXANDER MCQUEEN

40
Commits suicide at home

HUSSEIN CHALAYAN

DATE OF BIRTH
12 August 1970

BIRTHPLACE
Cyprus

LABEL
TSE, Puma, Chalayan

CAREER HIGHLIGHTS

Chalayan built his identity as one of the most intellectual and innovative designers of our time. Constantly experimenting with technology and art, he created "wow" moments with his statement shows and avant-garde designs, including a coffee table that turned into a wooden skirt. While his business went through financial ups and downs, the designer persevered, never letting his creative spirit waver.

1970

0
Born in Nicosia, Cyprus

Works with avant-garde musician Björk, who wears a jacket by the designer on the cover of her album "Post"

28
Sends 6 models down the runway of his AW98 show wearing only chadors, to make a statement about the oppression of Muslim women

Restructures his company and comes back with a new collection

32
Expands into menswear and launches a second, more affordable, line 2 years later

39
Collaborates with denim label J Brand on a line for women

Creative Director

Becomes creative director of Puma and sells a majority of his label's shares to the German sportswear company

$ No Hussein.
Chalayan

40
Buys back the shares of his label from Puma and changes his brand name to simply Chalayan

Opens his "I Am Sad Leyla" multimedia installation at the Lisson Gallery in London

8
Moves to the United Kingdom with his family

19
Studies design at Warwickshire College of Arts, and continues his training at Central Saint Martins

> I buried them for a few months.

23
His graduation collection, The Tangent Flows, is bought by influential British fashion boutique Browns

THE ABSOLUT CREATION AWARD
$ **$37,000 FUNDING**

Beats 100 competitors to take the top London fashion-design prize, The Absolut Creation Award, winning approximately US$37,000

hussein chalayan

25
Establishes his own company, Cartesia Ltd., and his ready-to-wear line, Hussein Chalayan

Becomes a design consultant for New York knitwear label TSE

30
Creates a remote-control dress, which premieres at the Hyères Festival in France

$ **$1.5 MILLION IN DEBT**

TSE terminates his contract, forcing his company into liquidation after accumulating debt of over US$1.5 million

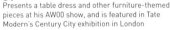

31
Presents a table dress and other furniture-themed pieces at his AW00 show, and is featured in Tate Modern's Century City exhibition in London

36
Presents a series of transformative dresses wired with hidden mechanisms for his SS07 collection

38
Collaborates with SHOWstudio on a film in which models wear Swarovski crystal-embellished dresses that emit lasers

"If you don't take risks in the world, nothing happens, you just stay static."

41
Launches a diffusion line, Grey Label, in a bid to reach new customers

VIONNET

45
Joins the creative team of French fashion brand Vionnet

> It's *Professor* Chalayan.

Becomes head professor of the fashion department at the University of Applied Arts, Vienna

NICOLAS GHESQUIÈRE

DATE OF BIRTH
9 May 1971

BIRTHPLACE
France

LABELS
Balenciaga, Louis Vuitton

1971

0
Born in Nord, France; his father owns a golf course

Starts to sketch clothing in his schoolbooks, and makes dresses out of his mother's curtains

Here's your pay!

agnès b.

14
Interns at Agnès B, and is paid in clothing

Bye.

BALENCIAGA
Creative Director

26
Promoted to creative director of Balenciaga, replacing Josephus Thimister

What?
No access?

Receives no access to the Balenciaga archives, and struggles to create buzz-worthy collections for his first few seasons

$
30 MILLION

Doubles the sales of Balenciaga to US$30 million after 2.5 years

29
Designs his first bag, the Motorcycle Lariat, which quickly becomes a bestseller

Balenciaga sucked me dry!

41
Leaves Balenciaga and takes a spiritual trip to Japan, shutting himself off from the media

"Fashion is a playground up until a certain age. But then you have to find your own signature and your own style."

LV
LOUIS VUITTON
Creative Director

42
Replaces Marc Jacobs as creative director of womenswear at Louis Vuitton

I love sports!

Enjoys sports including horse riding, fencing and swimming, which, later in life, inspires some of his designs

I want to be a designer...

Ghesquière takes to challenges like a duck to water. During his 15 years at the helm of Balenciaga, he drove the house forward with his clear, futuristic aesthetic. His talent for reinventing classics without losing the heart and heritage of the house makes him one of the greatest fashion talents of our time. His stellar reputation landed him the role of creative director at Louis Vuitton, where he continues to re-energize the fashion giant.

12
Decides to become a designer in order to do something different from his parents, and to alleviate boredom

Fashion is too hard for me...

Apprentices with designer Corinne Cobson for 2 years before going back to school

18
Moves to Paris to immerse himself in fashion

19
Leaves school and works as an assistant to Jean Paul Gaultier, learning the aesthetic of mixing styles

Many call it the worst position in fashion.

CallagHan

24
Works as a freelancer, designing mourning dresses for a Balenciaga licensee

22
Starts designing knitwear at Pôles, followed by a series of freelance design jobs, including at Callaghan, in Italy

91%

GUCCI

BALENCIAGA

Hired as a consultant for design house Callaghan to present a spring collection

30
The Gucci Group acquires a 91% share of Balenciaga, with Ghesquière owning the remaining 9%

33
Attracts a large number of young women who want to wear his signature slimline trousers

Sorry, no trousers!

38
Presents cocoon-shaped garments and fabrics in the SS09 collection

34
Chooses to show no trousers – the item of clothing for which he is famous – puzzling fashion editors

LAWSUIT

System

Nicolas Ghesquière

43
Presents his first collection for Louis Vuitton during AW14 Paris Fashion Week

Slapped with a lawsuit by Balenciaga for making derogatory comments about the brand in *System* magazine; the suit is settled out of court

45
Uses a fictional character, Lightning, from the game Final Fantasy, as the face of Louis Vuitton's AW16 campaign

STELLA McCARTNEY
STELLA NINA McCARTNEY

DATE OF BIRTH
13 September 1971

BIRTHPLACE
United Kingdom

LABELS
Chloé, Stella McCartney

1971

0
Born in London to ex-Beatle Paul McCartney and photographer, musician and animal-rights activist Linda McCartney

Chloé
Creative Director

26
Appointed creative director of Parisian fashion house Chloé, succeeding Karl Lagerfeld

STELLA McCARTNEY

30
Launches her eponymous fashion brand in a joint venture with the Gucci Group (now Kering), showing her first collection in Paris

36
Designs a limited-edition range available exclusively at 100 Target department stores in Australia

34
Designs an affordable collection for high-street giant H&M in order to reach a wider audience

Launches a 100% organic skincare line, CARE

37
Designs a limited-edition travel collection with LeSportsac

39
Collaborates with Disney on an "Alice in Wonderland"-inspired jewelry collection

"I'm real believer that just doing a little something is a lot better than doing a lot of nothing"

The Daily Telegraph
ONE OF BRITAIN'S MOST POWERFUL WOMEN

40
Named one of Britain's most powerful women by the *Telegraph*

43
Launches a sustainable eveningwear line, the Stella McCartney Green Carpet Collection

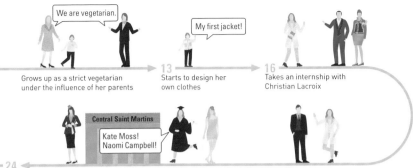

We are vegetarian.

My first jacket!

Grows up as a strict vegetarian under the influence of her parents

13 Starts to design her own clothes

16 Takes an internship with Christian Lacroix

Central Saint Martins

Kate Moss! Naomi Campbell!

24 Graduates from Central Saint Martins; her supermodel friends walk in her graduate runway show

Shadows Savile Row tailor Edward Sexton, her father's tailor for years, to improve her skills

32 Marries British entrepreneur Alasdhair Willis

33 Designs stage costumes for Madonna and Annie Lennox

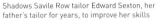

Collaborates with Adidas on a womenswear line, establishing a long-term partnership

— **CAREER HIGHLIGHTS** —

While today she is famous in her own right for her critically acclaimed brand and her animal-rights activism, McCartney's first steps into the world of fashion were overshadowed by the fame of her parents. Struggling to find her feet, her designs often ended up on worst-dressed lists. Her perseverance paid off, however, with her eco-friendly and vegan designs becoming some of the most sought-after in the world. She is also the only designer in the Kering Group to own an equal share in her business.

Works with PETA to petition the British Ministry of Defence to cease using Canadian black bear fur for the Royal Guards' hats

Appointed creative director of Adidas' 2012 Olympic and Paralympic Team GB ranges

Stella McCartney

PETA

Launches an anti-leather campaign with PETA ahead of London Fashion Week

Introduces the new iconic faux-leather Falabella handbag

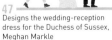

KERING

50% 50%

45 Debuts her first menswear collection

47 Designs the wedding-reception dress for the Duchess of Sussex, Meghan Markle

Buys back 50% of the Stella McCartney business from the Kering Group

RICCARDO TISCI

DATE OF BIRTH
1 August 1974

BIRTHPLACE
Italy

LABELS
Givenchy, Burberry

— CAREER HIGHLIGHTS —

Tisci was offered the coveted role of Givenchy creative director while he was still relatively unknown in the design world. Accepting it hesitantly in order to help his family, who were facing financial difficulties, he conjured up a fusion of gothic touches, Space Age minimalism and streetwear. Soon he reaped immense industry praise, drawing new attention to the brand. Tisci was also an early adopter of social media, harnessing the impact of influencers to lift the Givenchy brand, and his own name, onto the global stage.

1974

0

Born into a poor family in Taranto, in southern Italy

25

Returns to Italy, where he works for a number of brands including Antonio Berardi, Coccapani, and Puma

**3-YEAR CONTRACT
RUFFO RESEARCH**

Signs a 3-year contract with Ruffo Research, a business that collaborates with young designers

34

Named menswear and accessories designer of the Givenchy men's division

Designs costumes for Madonna and, later, Rihanna for their world tours

39

Sponsors the exhibition "PUNK: Chaos to Couture" at the Metropolitan Museum of Art in New York

His Rottweiler sweater, part of the AW11 collection, transforms the graphic sweater into a street style

She's the best!

Chooses Donatella Versace, head of Versace, to be the face of Givenchy's AW15 campaign

Designs "the very naked dress" for Beyoncé for the Met Gala; it is one of the most talked-about designs of the year

12 Works as a florist's assistant and a delivery boy to save money for art school abroad

Addicted to goth.

14 Experiments with dressing like a goth, and draws a lot of influence from his 8 sisters

17 Graduates from the Istituto d'Arte Applicata E Design in Cantù, Italy

Central Saint Martins

Wins a government grant to study at Central Saint Martins, where he meets his muse, MariaCarla Boscono, when she walks into his graduation show

Works as a shop assistant and in the studio of designer Antonio Berardi

Leaves Italy and moves to London to learn English

30 Spends time living in India and sets up his eponymous label

Debuts his first Riccardo Tisci collection in an off-calendar show with the help of Boscono

Now I can help my family.

GIVENCHY
Creative Director

Presents his first Givenchy haute couture collection in Paris. While poorly organized, his modernist vision is evident

31 Accepts role and puts his own label aside to help with his family's financial difficulties

Givenchy director?

Let me think...

Offered the role of creative director at Givenchy, though he is still relatively unknown

36 Casts the first transgender model, longtime assistant Lea T, in his catwalk show, causing a stir

37 Designs a leather kilt for Kanye West for his Watch the Throne tour; it becomes one of his most influential looks, and kick-starts the "under-layer" trend

> "I'm very faithful to myself. When you do things that are true, it just comes out quite instinctively."

I now wish to focus on my personal interests and passions.

43 Steps down as Givenchy creative director, though the house has expanded sixfold during his tenure

BURBERRY
CREATIVE OFFICER

44 Appointed creative officer of Burberry; debuts with a capsule collection, B Classic, and changes the delivery cycle

BURBERRY
LONDON ENGLAND

Unveils a new Burberry monogram and logo, in collaboration with Peter Saville

ICONIC ITEMS
BY DESIGNERS BORN DURING THE 1960s

1

TABLE DRESS – HUSSEIN CHALAYAN

Introduced in 2000
During his Fall/Winter 2000 show in London, the last model stepped into the middle of the table and lifted it up, transform it into a skirt. The show was inspired by refugees, who are forced to flee their homes taking only the possessions they can carry with them.

2

SKINNY SILHOUETTE – HEDI SLIMANE

Introduced in 2000
Famously inspiring Karl Lagerfeld to go on a diet, Hedi Slimane's skinny silhouette was so successful, it almost doubled Dior Homme's business volume and tripled Saint Laurent's sales.

3

FALABELLA BAG – STELLA McCARTNEY

Introduced in 2010
Following Stella McCartney's principle of not using materials made from animals, the Falabella went on to become one of the brand's bestselling pieces. It is also one of the most popular non-leather bags of all time.

4 SHRUNKEN SUIT – THOM BROWNE

Introduced in 2001

Thom Browne injected new life into the stale tailoring scene with this signature shrunken suit. Changing the proportions of the suit completely, Browne has been credited with revolutionizing the classic menswear staple.

5 OVERSIZED BOMBER JACKET – RAF SIMONS

Introduced in 2001

Raf Simons' Fall/Winter 2011 collection, Riot, Riot, Riot!, foreshadowed the international unrest surrounding the September 11 attacks. Seen on the likes of Rihanna and Kanye West, the oversized bomber jacket is one of the most sought-after items for any serious Raf Simons collector.

6 ARMADILLO HEELS – ALEXANDER McQUEEN

Introduced in 2009

McQueen's unusual Armadillo shoes referenced both armor and a ballerina *en pointe*. While the shoes were not intended to be produced commercially, some pairs were bought by adoring clients. Three pairs ended up at auction at Christie's in New York and sold for a combined total of US$295,000.

STATISTICS

Statistics can easily be overlooked. To help
spark ideas for your own unique fashion
journey, we compare the different choices and
events in the lives of the 50 legends in this book
using graphs and charts.

MAJOR SUBJECTS

Studying fashion design is not essential to becoming a designer.
In fact, a lot of legends planned to go into different professions, and
ended up switching gears without any formal fashion training.

3 DESIGNERS

Christian Dior
Emilio Pucci
Miuccia Prada

ART HISTORY

1 DESIGNER

Hedi Slimane

POLITICAL SCIENCE

MEDICINE

1 DESIGNER

Giorgio Armani

FASHION DESIGN

16 DESIGNERS

Alber Elbaz
Alexander McQueen
Calvin Klein
Cristóbal Balenciaga
Domenico Dolce
Donna Karan
Dries Van Noten
Hussein Chalayan

John Galliano
Kenzo Takada
Marc Jacobs
Michael Kors
Riccardo Tisci
Stella McCartney
Valentino Garavani
Yves Saint Laurent

1 DESIGNER

Yohji Yamamoto

LAW

10 DESIGNERS

Ann Demeulemeester	Martin Margiela
Azzedine Alaïa	Mary Quant
Franco Moschino	Oscar de la Renta
Hubert de Givenchy	Roberto Cavalli
Karl Lagerfeld	Rei Kawakubo

FINE ARTS
Painting/ Illustration/ Sculpture

BUSINESS AND ECONOMICS

1 DESIGNER

Vivienne Westwood

4 DESIGNERS

Diane von Furstenberg
Helmut Lang
Ralph Lauren
Thom Browne

SILVER-SMITHING

DESIGN

4 DESIGNERS

Issey Miyake
Jil Sander
Raf Simons
Stefano Gabbana

ARCHITECTURE

4 DESIGNERS

Gianni Versace
Pierre Balmain
Pierre Cardin
Tom Ford

1 DESIGNER

Karl Lagerfeld

HISTORY

OCCUPATION BEFORE DESIGNING

Not everyone in this book knew they wanted to be a fashion designer – some worked in entirely different fields before discovering their true calling.

SINGER
Coco Chanel

GALLERY OWNER
Christian Dior

SKIER
Emilio Pucci

WINDOW DRESSER
Sonia Rykiel

SALES ASSISTANT
Ralph Lauren

TEXTILE PRINTER
Roberto Cavalli

PRIMARY-SCHOOL TEACHER
Vivienne Westwood

TEXTILE COMPANY ADMINISTRATOR
Rei Kawakubo

STOCK BOY
Marc Jacobs

MIME
Miuccia Prada

FASHION ILLUSTRATOR
Franco Moschino

ADVERTISING
Stefano Gabbana

FASHION ILLUSTRATOR
Oscar de la Renta

WINDOW DRESSER
Giorgio Armani

MIDWIFE ASSISTANT
Azzedine Alaïa

PAINTER'S APPRENTICE
Kenzo Takada

FASHION JOURNALIST
Jil Sander

MENSWEAR BUYER
Paul Smith

PHOTOGRAPHER'S ASSISTANT
Diane von Furstenberg

WINDOW DRESSER
Donna Karan

SALESPERSON
Michael Kors

ACTOR
Tom Ford

FINANCIAL CONSULTANT
Thom Browne

FURNITURE DESIGNER
Raf Simons

DEBUT SHOW CITY

Paris is still the city of fashion. A common theme among these legends is launching their brand in Paris, no matter the decade in which they were born.

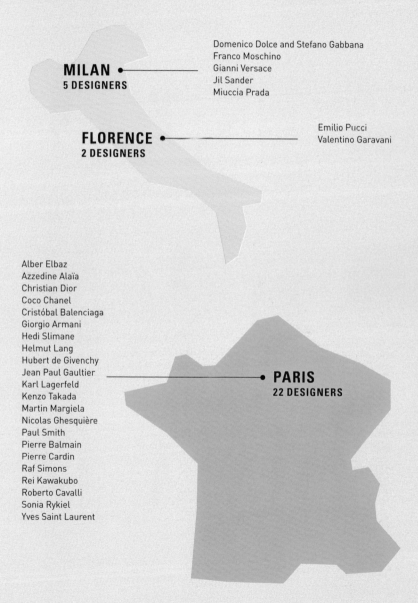

MILAN
5 DESIGNERS

Domenico Dolce and Stefano Gabbana
Franco Moschino
Gianni Versace
Jil Sander
Miuccia Prada

FLORENCE
2 DESIGNERS

Emilio Pucci
Valentino Garavani

Alber Elbaz
Azzedine Alaïa
Christian Dior
Coco Chanel
Cristóbal Balenciaga
Giorgio Armani
Hedi Slimane
Helmut Lang
Hubert de Givenchy
Jean Paul Gaultier
Karl Lagerfeld
Kenzo Takada
Martin Margiela
Nicolas Ghesquière
Paul Smith
Pierre Balmain
Pierre Cardin
Raf Simons
Rei Kawakubo
Roberto Cavalli
Sonia Rykiel
Yves Saint Laurent

PARIS
22 DESIGNERS

TOKYO
1 DESIGNER

Yohji Yamamoto

Alexander McQueen
Ann Demeulemeester
Dries Van Noten
Hussein Chalayan
John Galliano
Mary Quant

Riccardo Tisci
Stella McCartney
Vivienne Westwood

LONDON
9 DESIGNERS

NEW YORK
11 DESIGNERS

Calvin Klein
Diane von Furstenberg
Donna Karan
Issey Miyake
Marc Jacobs
Michael Kors
Oscar de la Renta
Ralph Lauren
Thom Browne
Tom Ford
Tommy Hilfiger

AGE OF OPENING FIRST STORE

When it comes to opening your first store, there is no optimal time. These legends all opened stores at entirely different ages.

Oscar de la Renta (72 / New York)
Karl Lagerfeld (80 / Paris)

Diane von Furstenberg (51 / New York)
Azzedine Alaïa (53 / Paris)

Donna Karan (46 / London)
Tom Ford (46 / New York)
Giorgio Armani (47 / Milan)
Michael Kors (47 / New York)

Christian Dior (41 / Paris)
Martin Margiela (43 / Tokyo)
John Galliano (43 / Paris)
Hussein Chalayan (45 / London)

Emilio Pucci (36 / Capri)
Issey Miyake (36 / Tokyo)
Miuccia Prada (36 / Milan)
Yohji Yamamoto (37 / Tokyo)
Valentino Garavani (37 / Milan)
Thom Browne (38 / New York)
Sonia Rykiel (38 / Paris)
Franco Moschino (39 / Milan)
Raf Simons (40 / Tokyo)
Ann Demeulemeester (40 / Antwerp)

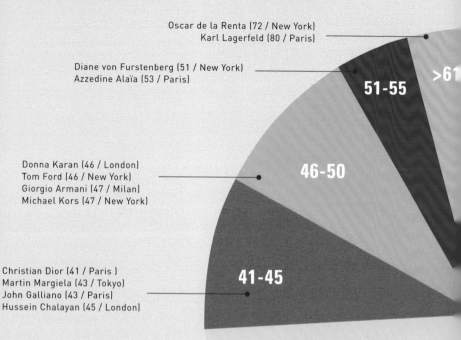

>61

51-55

46-50

41-45

36-40

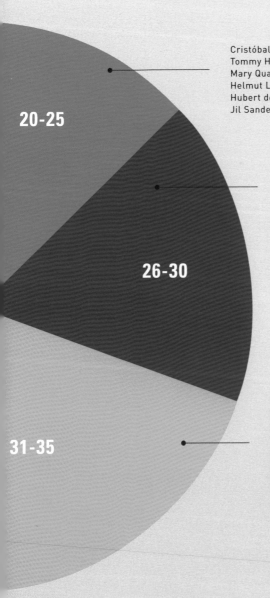

20-25

Cristóbal Balenciaga (20 / San Sebastián)
Tommy Hilfiger (20 / New York)
Mary Quant (21 / London)
Helmut Lang (23 / Vienna)
Hubert de Givenchy (25 / Paris)
Jil Sander (25 / Germany)

26-30

Domenico Dolce & Stefano Gabbana
(25,29 / Milan)
Calvin Klein (26 / New York)
Coco Chanel (27 / Paris)
Dries Van Noten (28 / Antwerp)
Vivienne Westwood (29 / London)
Stella McCartney (30 / New York)
Jean Paul Gaultier (30 / Paris)
Yves Saint Laurent (30 / Paris)

31-35

Kenzo Takada (31 / Paris)
Ralph Lauren (31 / New York)
Pierre Cardin (32 / Paris)
Roberto Cavalli (32 / Saint-Tropez)
Gianni Versace (32 / Milan)
Rei Kawakubo (33 / Tokyo)
Paul Smith (33 / London)
Marc Jacobs (34 / New York)
Alexander McQueen (34 / London)
Pierre Balmain (35 / New York)

FAILURES AND SUCCESSES

Fashion is not an easy business. It is easy to fall, but a fashion legend can always find a way to get back on their feet.

CHRISTIAN DIOR

Dior's gallery closed due to the depression and bankruptcy of his father, but he went on to present the iconic New Look, which marked the start of his fashion empire.

YOHJI YAMAMOTO

Yamamoto's brand had debts of more than US$65 million due to poor financial decisions. But he was able to clear it after restructuring his business in 2010.

RALPH LAUREN

Lauren's inexperience in managing the finances and logistics of his business almost caused him to go bankrupt. But he soon got back on his feet, and his company went public not long after.

+42.37 (+0.28%)

COCO CHANEL

Chanel's couture house was forced to shut down due to WWII. But she returned with a new version of the tweed jacket, and found great success in the American market.

JOHN GALLIANO

Galliano was fired by Christian Dior after he was caught making anti-Semitic remarks in a Paris bar. But he returned as creative director of Maison Margiela.

America

I am guilty...

NICOLAS GHESQUIÈRE

Ghesquière designed not-so-glamorous golf and funeral clothes for a Balenciaga licensee that he claims "many would call the worst position in fashion". But later he became creative director of the house, and rebuilt it through fresh innovation.

BALENCIAGA
Creative Director

TOMMY HILFIGER

Hilfiger's first shop, The People's Place, went bankrupt when he was only 25. But he learned quickly, and soon became one of America's most celebrated menswear designers.

ALBER ELBAZ

Elbaz was forced to leave Yves Saint Laurent when Tom Ford became creative director. But later he made the dying house of Lanvin one of the most sought-after brands.

CALVIN KLEIN

Klein presented controversial ads that caused plenty of negative press – he even had charges made against him. But he soon returned with excellent sales and profits.

VALENTINO GARAVANI

Valentino faced bankruptcy just 1 year after the start of his business, but managed to turn it around with an international debut – and a large order from Jackie Kennedy.

FAILURES AND SUCCESSES – CONT'D

HUSSEIN CHALAYAN

Chalayan was US$1.5 million in debt and was forced to go into voluntary liquidation. But he restructured the company and staged a comeback collection.

YVES SAINT LAURENT

Yves Saint Laurent was fired by Dior during his military service, but then soon saw huge success with a signature collection under his own house.

$1.5 MILLION IN DEBT

I've been fired.

Christian Dior

MARC JACOBS

Jacobs enjoyed critical acclaim for his grunge collection in 1992. But he was still fired due to its lack of commercial success. He later became famous for turning the luggage-only brand Louis Vuitton into a powerful fashion house.

ART DIRECTOR

DOMENICO DOLCE & STEFANO GABBANA

The duo was charged and convicted of tax evasion in 2013, and they were threatened with having to return their City of Milan Ambrogino Gold Medal. However, they appealed successfully and overturned their conviction in 2014.

TAX EVASION

TURNOVER OF A HOUSE

There have been several incredibly talented designers who have managed to inject new energy and sales into historic houses, bringing them back to the global stage.

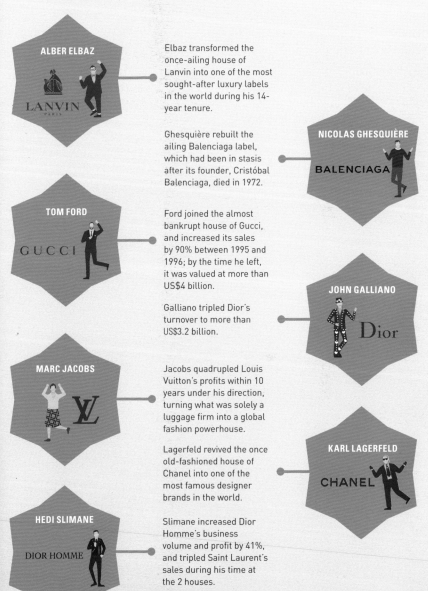

ALBER ELBAZ

LANVIN
PARIS

Elbaz transformed the once-ailing house of Lanvin into one of the most sought-after luxury labels in the world during his 14-year tenure.

Ghesquière rebuilt the ailing Balenciaga label, which had been in stasis after its founder, Cristóbal Balenciaga, died in 1972.

NICOLAS GHESQUIÈRE

BALENCIAGA

TOM FORD

GUCCI

Ford joined the almost bankrupt house of Gucci, and increased its sales by 90% between 1995 and 1996; by the time he left, it was valued at more than US$4 billion.

Galliano tripled Dior's turnover to more than US$3.2 billion.

JOHN GALLIANO

Dior

MARC JACOBS

LV

Jacobs quadrupled Louis Vuitton's profits within 10 years under his direction, turning what was solely a luggage firm into a global fashion powerhouse.

Lagerfeld revived the once old-fashioned house of Chanel into one of the most famous designer brands in the world.

KARL LAGERFELD

CHANEL

HEDI SLIMANE

DIOR HOMME

Slimane increased Dior Homme's business volume and profit by 41%, and tripled Saint Laurent's sales during his time at the 2 houses.

DESIGNERS WHO LEFT THEIR OWN BRANDS

Not every fashion designer works on their brand their entire lives. These legends left their eponymous labels, and allowed them to be run by other people.

DONNA KARAN   AGE / 67

> I want to focus on my lifestyle brand, Urban Zen.

DKNY
DONNA KARAN NEW YORK

KENZO TAKADA   AGE / 60

> It's time for me to retire. My assistant can take care of the house.

KENZO

VALENTINO GARAVANI   AGE / 75

> My future will be filled with new interests and challenges!

VALENTINO

JIL SANDER   AGE / 57 / 61 / 70

> I had insurmountable differences with Prada's chief executive, Patrizio Bertelli.

JIL SANDER

ISSEY MIYAKE   AGE / 61

I want to focus on experimenting!

ISSEY MIYAKE

YVES SAINT LAURENT   AGE / 66

I'm exhausted and depressed.

HELMUT LANG   AGE / 49

I became an artist.

HELMUT LANG

MARTIN MARGIELA   AGE / 52

...

Maison Margiela
PARIS

JOHN GALLIANO   AGE / 51

I was fired.

John Galliano

ANN DEMEULEMEESTER   AGE / 45

The brand is mature enough to run without me.

ANN DEMEULEMEESTER

WISDOM

"Success is often achieved by those who don't know that failure is inevitable."

COCO CHANEL

"Rules are invented for lazy people who don't want to think for themselves."

MARY QUANT

"Remain true to yourself and your philosophy."

GIORGIO ARMANI

"For something to be beautiful it doesn't have to be pretty."

REI KAWAKUBO

"Anything I wanted to do, I did. If there's something I want to do, nothing stops me."

CALVIN KLEIN

"Don't dress for fashion, dress for yourself."

PAUL SMITH

"Good taste doesn't exist. It is our taste. We have to be proud of it."

FRANCO MOSCHINO

"Always stay focused. Always give and try your best."

TOMMY HILFIGER

"I react against everything that's chic and traditional. If you don't revolt, then you don't go anywhere." **MARTIN MARGIELA**

"Our role is to dream and inspire rather than collude in impacting the reality." **DRIES VAN NOTEN**

"You only get a short life, so take chances." **JOHN GALLIANO**

"It is so important to be really true to yourself in design, and I am." **THOM BROWNE**

"If you don't take risks in the world, nothing happens, you just stay static." **HUSSEIN CHALAYAN**

"Fashion is a playground up until a certain age. But then you have to find your own signature and your own style." **NICOLAS GHESQUIÈRE**

"I'm a real believer that just doing a little something is a lot better than doing a lot of nothing." **STELLA McCARTNEY**

"I'm very faithful to myself. When you do things that are true, it just comes out quite instinctively." **RICCARDO TISCI**

REFERENCES

WEBSITES

500nomore.com
90srunway.tumblr.com
acontinuouslean.com
addicted2success.com
agentofstyle.com
agnautacouture.com
agoraclothing.com
alaia.fr
alexandermcqueen.com
allure.com
allwomenstalk.com
angelasancartier.net
anndemeulemeester.com
annuaire-createurs.fr
anothermag.com
anothertravelguide.com
ans-wer.com
answers.com
antwerpart.be
apieceoftoastblog.com
archive.fortune.com
archive.is
artandsmoke.com
artnet.com
artpartner.com
artsandculture.google.com
askmen.com
awhitecarousel.com
azquotes.com
balmain.com
barneys.com
basquetribune.com
bazaarvietnam.vn
bbc.com
bbook.com
beautimode.com
beautyandtips.com
beaverbrooks.co.uk
bijog.com
billboard.com
biography.com
blog.courtauld.ac.uk
blog.kitmeout.com
blog.momu.be
blog.viviennewestwood.com

bloomberg.com
bornrich.com
brainyquote.com
brandchannel.com
brides.com
britannica.com
brownthomas.com
buro247.me
businessinsider.com
businessoffashion.com
bykoket.com
cahierdexercices.com
cameramoda.it
carolineleaper.com
carrehomme.fr
catwalkyourself.com
cdn-fashionschool.pressidium.com
cdn.stylefrizz.com
celebfamily.com
celine.com
chanel-news.chanel.com
childrenofthenineties.blogspot.com
cn.businessoffashion.com
cn.fashionnetwork.com
cnn.com
collegefashion.net
comfortingquotes.com
complex.com
cosmopolitan.com.hk
countryandtownhouse.co.uk
crfashionbook.com
cristobalbalenciagamuseoa.com
crunchbase.com
culturedivine.com
dailymail.co.uk
dailymotion.com
dazeddigital.com
denverpost.com
designer-vintage.com
dezeen.com
dineshree9.wordpress.com
dior-finance.com
dior.com
dirty-mag.com
doctorleatherph.com

WEBSITES

indobase.com
influentialdesigners.weebly.com
inhabitat.com
inspiringquotes.us
instyle.com
interviewmagazine.com
israel21c.org
isseymiyake.com
issuu.com
izquotes.com
jeanpaulgaultier.com
jiemian.com
johngalliano.com
kaneesha.com
karl.com
kci.or.jp
kering.com
Lapouyette-unddiedingedeslebens.
blogspot.hk
lifehack.org
lifestyle.inquirer.net
london.doverstreetmarket.com
loveparisloveparis.wordpress.com
luxe.co
luxottica.com
lvmh.com
m.imdb.com
mad-eyes.net
maisonmargiela.com
marieclaire.co.uk
marieclaire.com
marieclaire.com.my
maripiermorin.com
marybawa.in
medium.com
meetthedesigner.co.uk
meltingbutter.com
metmuseum.org
michaelkors.com
mightygoods.com
milano.corriere.it
mings.mpweekly.com
mirror.co.uk
mocoloco.com
mod-tv.com

modartmbafashion.wordpress.com
moma.org
moschino.com
museeyslparis.com
mycloset.com
myuniquestylemh-monisha.blogspot.com
nact.jp
neimanmarcus.com
newsfeed.time.com
newsweck.com
newworldencyclopedia.org
newyorker.com
nipponcouture.com
nofashion.cn
notable-quotes.com
notablebiographies.com
nymag.com
nyt.com
nytimes.com
observer.com
onobello.com
pagesix.com
papercitymag.com
paris-shanghai-fashion.com
people.com
philatelynews.com
phillystylemag.com
pierrecardin.com
pilikabobolinabebeludo.wordpress.com
pinterest.com
pleasurephoto.wordpress.com
port-magazine.com
prabook.com
prada.com
pradagroup.com
prezi.com
purseblog.com
queensofvintage.com
quotesgram.com
quotlr.com
rafsimons.com
reed.edu
referenceforbusiness.com
refinery29.com
reuters.com

richemont.com
ris.fashion.telegraph.co.uk
rizzoliusa.com
row.jimmychoo.com
rykielism.soniarykiel.com
salutemag.com
sandbridgecap.com
sassisamblog.com
schoolofstyle.com
scmp.com
shefinds.com
shelflife.co.za
showstudio.com
shutterstock.com
sleek-mag.com
smagazineofficial.com
smh.com.au
soberrecovery.com
somethingaboutmagazine.com
soniarykiel.com
spainisculture.com
sparklesandshoes.com
spindlemagazine.com
ssense.com
standard.co.uk
stellamccartney.com
stylezeitgeist.com
stylist.co.uk
successstory.com
susananakatani.com
sz-mag.com
teampeterstigter.com
techspot.com
teenvogue.com
telegraph.co.uk
the-widows-of-culloden.tumblr.com
theageofgrace.com
thecurrentdaily.com
thecut.com
thedailybeast.com
thefamouspeople.com
thefancyarchive.com
thefashionisto.com
thefashionlaw.com
thefashionspot.com

thefashiontalk.wordpress.com
theguardian.com
theidleman.com
thelondoner.me
themadameblue.com
theperfumemagazine.com
theredlist.com
thesteepletimes.com
thesun.co.uk
thewildmagazine.com
thewindow.barneys.com
thinkfashion.com
thombrowne.com
thoughtco.com
time.com
tmagazine.blogs.nytimes.com
today.com
tokyoartbeat.com
tomford.com
topteny.com
trendwalk.net
tw.appledaily.com
tw.fashionnetwork.com
uk.dvf.com
uk.fashionnetwork.com
uncrated.wordpress.com
universityoffashion.com
upclosed.com
us.fashionnetwork.com
uselessdaily.com
valentinogaravanimuseum.com
valiram.com
vam.ac.uk
vanityfair.com
versace.com
vestoj.com
vintagedancer.com
visionaireworld.com
vogue.co.uk
vogue.com
vogue.it
vox.com
washingtonpost.com
whatgrandmawore.com
whitehill-sec.glasgow.sch.uk

WEBSITES

whitewall.art
whowhatwear.com
wmagazine.com
womenworkforce.weebly.com
world.dvf.com
wsj.com
wwd.com
xinhuanet.com
yohjiyamamoto.co.jp
zacposen.com
zhihu.com

BOOKS

100 Contemporary Fashion Designers
Terry Jones, James Anderson
Köln: Taschen

100 Ideas That Changed Fashion: Calvin Klein
Underwear: Jock Straps and Boxer Shorts for
Girls (Idea No 83)
London: Laurence King

A Century of Fashion
François Baudot
New York: Universe

A Magazine #1
curated by Maison Martin Margiela
Antwerp: A Publisher for Flanders Fashion
Institute

Alaïa
Michel Tournier, Azzedine Alaïa, Juan Gatti,
Sophie Djerlal, Martine Barrat
Göttingen: Steidl

Alexander McQueen
Claire Wilcox, Victoria and Albert Museum
London: V&A

Alexander McQueen: Savage Beauty
Andrew Bolton, Alexander McQueen,
Susannah Frankel, Tim Blanks, Sølve Sundsbø
Metropolitan Museum of Art (New York)
New York: Metropolitan Museum of Art

Alexander McQueen: the Life and the Legacy
Judith Watt
New York: Harper Design

All-American: a Style Book
Tommy Hilfiger
New York: Universe

Ann Demeulemeester
Patti Smith, Ann Demeulemeester
New York: Rizzoli

Balenciaga Paris
Pamela Golbin, Fabien Baron, Musée de la mode
et du textile
New York: Thames & Hudson

Balenciaga: Shaping Fashion
Lesley Ellis Miller, Victoria and Albert Museum,
South Kensington Museum, Science Museum
(Great Britain), Museum of Ornamental Art
London: V&A

B magazine, issue no.54
Korea: Suyong Joh

Calvin Klein
Calvin Klein
New York: Rizzoli

Christian Dior
Richard Martin (Richard Harrison), Harold Koda
& Metropolitan Museum of Art (New York)
New York: Metropolitan Museum of Art

Christian Dior: the Biography
Marie-France Pochna
New York: Overlook Duckworth

Coco Chanel: a Biography
Axel Madsen
London: Bloomsbury

**Cristóbal Balenciaga: the Making of a Master
(1895-1936)**
Miren Arzalluz
London: V&A

**Dior: 60 Years of Style from Christian Dior to
John Galliano**
Farid Chenoune, Laziz Hamani
London: Thames & Hudson

Dior by Dior: the Autobiography of Christian Dior
Christian Dior
London: Weidenfeld & Nicolson

Dries Van Noten
Geert Bruloot, Pamela Golbin, Joseph Logan,
Dries Van Noten, Musée des arts décoratifs
(France), Modemuseum Provincie Antwerpen
Tielt, Belgium: Lannoo Publishers

Emilio Pucci
Katell Le Bourhis, Stefania Ricci, Luigi
Settembrini, Palazzo Pitti, Biennale di Firenze
Milano: Skira

Emilio Pucci
Mariuccia Casadio, Elizabeth Currie
London: Thames and Hudson

**Fashion: 150 Years, Couturiers, Designers,
Labels**
Charlotte Seeling
Köln: H.F. Ullmann Publishing GmbH

Fashion Visionaries
Linda Watson
London: Laurence King

Giorgio Armani
Giorgio Armani
New York: Rizzoli

Haute Couture Ateliers: the Artisans of Fashion
Hélène Farnault, Hubert de Givenchy, Alexis
Lecomte, Lorna Dale
New York: Vendome Press

**Hello, My Name Is Paul Smith: Fashion and
Other Stories**
Paul Smith, Deyan Sudjic, Donna Loveday,
Alan Aboud, Design Museum (London, England)
New York: Rizzoli

Hussein Chalayan
Robert Violette, Judith Clark
New York: Rizzoli

Hussein Chalayan
Hussein Chalayan, Caroline Evans, Groninger
Museum
Rotterdam: NAI

Issey Miyake
Marie-Andrée Jouve
New York: Universe

BOOKS

Jean Paul Gaultier
Colin McDowell
London: Cassell

Jean Paul Gaultier
Farid Chenoune
London: Thames and Hudson

John Galliano: Unseen
Robert Fairer and Claire Wilcox
London: Thames & Hudson

Kenzo
Ginette Sainderichin, Elizabeth Currie
New York: Universe

Lanvin: I Love You
Alber Elbaz
New York: Rizzoli

Mademoiselle: Coco Chanel and the Pulse of History
Rhonda K. Garelick
New York: Random House

Mary Quant: Autobiography
Mary Quant
London: Headline

Maison Martin Margiela
Maison Martin Margiela
New York: Rizzoli

My Journey
Donna Karan
New York: Ballantine Books

Pierre Cardin: the Man Who Became a Label
Richard Morais
London: Bantam

Pierre Cardin Evolution: Furniture and Design
Benjamin Loyauté, Jérôme Faggiano,
Nils Herrmann
Paris: Flammarion

Pierre Cardin: 60 Years of Innovation
Jean-Pascal Hesse, Laurence Benaïm
New York: Assouline

Raf Simons: Designer Monographs
Raf Simons, Terry Jones
Köln: Taschen

Raf Simons: Redux
Peter De Potter, Raf Simons, Maria Luisa Frisa
Milano: Charta

Ralph Lauren
Ralph Lauren
New York: Rizzoli

Ralph Lauren: the Man, the Vision, the Style
Colin McDowell
London: Cassell Illustrated

Rei Kawakubo/Comme des Garçons: Art of the In-Between
Andrew Bolton
New York: Metropolitan Museum of Art

Rei Kawakubo: Designer Monographs
Rei Kawakubo, Terry Jones
Köln: Taschen

Roberto Cavalli
Roberto Cavalli, Mert Alas, Marcus Piggott
New York: Rizzoli

Schiaparelli & the Artists
Daniel Melamud
New York: Rizzoli

Sonia Rykiel
Patrick Mauriès
New York: Universe

Talking to Myself
Yohji Yamamoto, Kiyokazu Washida,
Carla Sozzani
Göttingen: Steidl

The Givenchy Style
Françoise Mohrt
New York: Vendome Press

The Naked & the Dressed: 20 Years of Versace
Richard Avedon, Gianni Versace
London: Random House

The New French Couture: Icons of Paris Fashion
Elyssa Dimant
New York: Harper Design

The Study of Comme des Garçons
Minamitani Eriko, Akiyama Michio
Tokyo: Ritoru Moa

Tom Ford
Tom Ford, Bridget Foley, Graydon Carter,
Anna Wintour
New York: Rizzoli

Valentino
Valentino, Franca Sozzani, Luca Stoppini
New York: Rizzoli

Valentino
Bernadine Morris
London: Thames and Hudson

Versace
Richard Harrison Martin
London: Thames and Hudson

Versace
Mariuccia Casadio, Samuele Mazza
London: Thames and Hudson

Vivienne Westwood
Claire Wilcox
London: V&A

Vivienne Westwood
Vivienne Westwood, Ian Kelly
London: Picador

X Years of Kaos, 1983-1993
Franco Moschino, Lida Castelli
Milano: Edizioni Lybra Immagine

Yamamoto & Yohji
Yohji Yamamoto, Susannah Frankel
New York: Rizzoli

Yohji Yamamoto: My Dear Bomb
山本耀司，滿田愛，陳品秀
台北市 : 行人文化實驗室

Yohji Yamamoto: Designer Monographs
Yohji Yamamoto, Terry Jones
Köln: Taschen

You Can Find Inspiration in Everything*
*And If You Can't, Look Again
Paul Smith
London: Violette Editions

Yves Saint Laurent
Pierre Bergé, Richard Neel
London: Thames and Hudson

Yves Saint Laurent
Yves Saint Laurent, Diana Vreeland, Costume
Institute (New York)
Thames: Metropolitan Museum of Art

ACKNOWLEDGMENTS

CHAIRMAN Penter Yip

EDITOR-IN-CHIEF Charlotte Chan

EDITOR Jane Kwan
Sara Chow

ILLUSTRATOR & Good Morning Design
LAYOUT DESIGN

EDITING Karmuel Young
CONSULTANT

COPY EDITOR Lisa Burnett Hillman
English Editorial Solutions

RESEARCHERS Charlene Wong
Rachel Fong
Rosa Lo
Yoyo Tsang

CONTRIBUTORS We would like to thank all the contributors who
provided us their sincere feedback and helped
us improve this book along the way. We could not
have done it without them.

Christopher Lai
David Yiu
Haylee Wong
Jennifer Wong
Jessica Yang
Julie J.Y. Chun
Kevin Wong
Kit Lo
Lammy Chan
Noel Lai
Ronnie Tung
Steve Wan
Vikki Yau
Yin Hui